GRAVITY *the allure of distance*

GRAVITY *the allure of distance*

ESSAYS ON THE ACT OF TRAVEL

W. Scott Olsen

THE UNIVERSITY OF UTAH PRESS
Salt Lake City

The Defiance House Man colophon is a registered trademark of The University of Utah Press. It is based upon a four-foot-tall Ancient Puebloan pictograph (late PIII) near Glen Canyon, Utah.

Permission to reprint from *Kawe Korero: A Guide to Reporting Maori Activities*, courtesy of the author, Michael King.

"Pointed Home" was first published by Pecan Grove Press, San Antonio, Texas, as *Pointed Home: A Cross-Country Essay*. Permission to reprint courtesy of Pecan Grove Press.

Printed on acid-free paper

08 07 06 05 04 03

5 4 3 2 1

LIBRARY OF CONGRESS CATALOGING-IN-PUBLICATION DATA

Olsen, W. Scott, 1958–
  Gravity, the allure of distance : essays on the act of travel /
W. Scott Olsen
    p. cm.
ISBN 0-87480-749-2 (pbk. : alk. paper)
1. Olsen, W. Scott, 1958—Journeys. 2. Voyages and travels.
I. Title
  G465 .O47 2003
  910.4—dc21

                      2003001199

for Maureen and Kate and Andrew

CONTENTS

ACKNOWLEDGMENTS

I owe a significant debt to many people for their help with this book, and to each of them I am profoundly grateful. Concordia College, the Lake Region Arts Council, and the Jerome Foundation each provided funding to help with the cost of travel. Peter Chilson, Lin Enger, Bill Kloefkorn, Doug Carlson, and Jim and Eleanor Coomber have all been generous readers of early drafts. Annette Wenda carefully attended every sentence. Mark Monmonier was an invaluable resource with my map questions. Information about medieval maps and the monsters within them came from John Block Friedman's wonderful book, *The Monstrous Races in Medieval Art and Thought*. Gary Moulton's multivolume edition of *The Journals of Lewis and Clark* informed and continues to sustain my understanding of the act of travel. Early versions of these essays appeared in the journals *Weber Studies, North Dakota Quarterly, Amarillo Bay, Salt River Review, Del Sol Review, The Tampa Review,* and *River Teeth*, as well as in the books *The Sacred Place, When We Say We're Home* (both The University of Utah Press), and *Pointed Home* (Pecan Grove Press). Dawn Marano, my editor at

The University of Utah Press, has been, as before, a patient, brilliant, and insistent friend to this work. Without the help of these people and organizations, as well as the openness of the great many people I've met on the road and who appear in these pages, this book would not be possible.

INTRODUCTION

Essays on the Act of Travel

IMAGINE NORTHERN MINNESOTA, LATE SUMMER, LATE AT NIGHT. Highway 200 between Floodwood and Jacobson is a dark path of broken asphalt lit by a waxing moon. On either side of the road, the forests absorb the meager light and nearly radiate blackness. This is remote country. And imagine an old Jeep on this road, heading west. This is my Jeep, and this story is true. I was driving.

Highway 200 is a road I know well. It's part of a route that takes me from my home on the Dakota border to a place called Wolf Ridge, an hour out of Duluth on the North Shore of Lake Superior. It's important to say I know this road, because on this particular night, I was thinking precisely about this road. I was happy, per-haps even smug, about my knowledge. I knew the turns. I knew the holes. I knew where the deer would be. I knew the smell, and the sound, and the sight. I was wondering if I could include this road in the idea I called home, and I was remembering this road in other seasons—in hard cold, in rain, in midday summer heat, in wool-thick fog. I was telling myself that I knew the history here. And then an owl flew out of the woods.

Let's put the story in present tense, because that's the way it feels. An owl flies out of the woods. And not just any owl, but a great gray owl, an owl the guidebooks call huge, with a wingspan of five feet. Yellow eyes. It flies low, fast, diving, chasing something that will keep it alive. But there is a brightness to its left and so it turns, not away, but toward the unexpected. The unexpected, of course, is the front of my Jeep, rushing toward this owl at sixty miles per hour.

I'll give away the ending. The owl pulled up and over the Jeep. Not even a single feather was grazed. But the important moment here has nothing to do with the meeting of owl and grill or windshield. The important moment is somewhere in the turn of the owl, when a pattern it knew instinctively—the chase of a mouse or whatever in a landscape it knew intimately from its own history— was hard broken, and fast, by something unexpected. The important moment is in the turn of the owl, when what I saw for the briefest fraction of a second was a face, a pair of eyes looking straight into mine (though I'm certain all the owl could see were the lights of the onrushing Jeep). The important moment is in the turn of the owl, when both owl and human, both comfortable in a routine they knew well, had that comfort exploded, and then reassembled. The important moment is the one where the unexpected becomes the possible, where depth of knowledge meets new experience, and reorders everything.

We are a species that loves to move. We do not migrate, in the normal sense of the word, moving from one part of the globe to another in search of food or safe haven for breeding. But we have a very hard time staying put. We go to visit relatives. We go on vacation. We hit the road when routine becomes oppressive. We celebrate speed with fast cars, fast food, fast computers to bring us the world. We make myths and legends from the stories the travelers bring home. There is a pull to the universe, an insistent something that calls us out, then over, then across. On the road, there is always the chance the world will be unmade for us, and then remade larger.

This is a book about gravity, the allure of distance, the attraction of the far away. And while many books are about the other places, this is not one of them. This is a book about the act of going. This is a road book where something happens, or doesn't, where you see something, or don't, and suddenly the world is a lot larger than our easy everyday understanding, borders of landscape and history and imagination are fluid if not meaningless, and words like *possibility* and *grace* seem better than most. This is a book about movement, about the road, and the hope for the sudden turn of an owl.

THE LOVE OF MAPS

"So," I ask him. "Why are *you* here?"

I am standing with Martin Tobias at the Klondike Korner, at the beginning of the Dempster Highway, in the Yukon Territory. Overhead, the sun is bright and warm. Both of us are smiling. A hundred yards to our north, a small single-lane bridge crosses the Klondike River where bright-red salmon break the surface of the shallow, tumbling stream. I have stopped at this corner to gather my breath, my luck, my courage. This is the beginning of the end, the last road, the road I'd heard stories about more than two thousand miles away, the fundamental reason I am here. A sign tells me, "The Dempster is the only public highway in North America that crosses the Arctic Circle; beyond this point is a world that many of you will have never seen." Another sign, labeled "Some Tips for Travellers," says, "Don't Forget! In summer, bring: mosquito repellent, first aid kit, water carrier, emergency flares, spare gas."

I can taste the adrenaline.

I had watched a light-blue minivan rumble over the bridge and come to a stop by the sign. A bearded man, heavyset, somewhere in his forties, got out, took a breath. At the beginning and the end of the Dempster Highway, more than seven hundred kilometers of single-lane gravel traversing Arctic tundra, two large rivers, and a half-dozen mountain ranges, with only Eagle Plains, the halfway point, providing gasoline, maintenance, and food, introductions are easy. Tobias is from Oregon. Not so long ago, he stood and wondered what would come after this bridge.

"So," I ask him. "Why are *you* here?"

"Oh," he answers me with a grin, "I saw it on a map."

1

BEGIN IN YOUR DRIVEWAY.

Don't get killed.

Put the car, the truck, the minivan in a forward gear, and there it is. Somewhere just beyond the first stop sign, somewhere in the back of your brain, somewhere in the "If just a few things were different . . . " you hear that voice. Keep going, it says. Pass the day care, the grocery store, the job site, the office. Just keep your foot on the floor. This road ends somewhere, and you don't know where that somewhere is.

There is a connection already. Pavement runs from your driveway to New York, to Key West, to the Bay of Fundy, to the tall grass prairies, to glaciers and deserts and evening-time stories you have not heard. You've followed the red and blue map lines at rest stops, on gas station walls, in your own garage. As if you've put your head to railroad tracks to hear an oncoming train, you can feel the faraway places in your tires.

So go! Begin in your driveway. Don't get killed.

2

THIS STORY, LIKE ALL STORIES, BEGINS WITH A MAP.

While this particular road trip begins with countless hours spent over an old and coverless, dog-eared, coffee-stained edition of a *Rand McNally Road Atlas*—wondering where roads began and ended, needing to know how to get from Fargo to Charlottesville, imagining myself toward Glacier National Park, toward Crater Lake, toward the Tetons and then the Blue Ridge Mountains, tracing my fingers over the lines that mean highway, county road, and gravel leading from home to anywhere and everywhere else—the story of this trip begins much earlier, in the Middle Ages, when the corners of the world had not been seen and mapmakers believed in monsters.

The story of this trip begins with a map, which is to say the story of this trip begins with a need.

3

I BEGIN IN MY DRIVEWAY. Start the very old Jeep. Back out, turn right under the midsummer canopy of bright-green elm leaves. The early morning dew still beaded in the moss on the trunks. These trees are fragile, as old as any on the midwestern prairie. Each day, I find myself touching at least one of them, a physical contact with the things surrounding my home.

Put the Jeep in first gear. The neighborhood is quiet, hushed in the way that a room filled with people can be quieter than the same room empty. In a few hours, every doorway and driveway here will issue people toward work, school, the routines and patterns of everyday living. But now, the houses and yards only glimmer in the new daylight. Ready.

Roll south. Stop at the stop sign. Turn left onto Seventh Avenue. On the right, the college dormitory shimmers as an early morning thunderstorm has just left town, and the threshold between campus lawn and building wall still seems fluid. Robins and sparrows and nuthatches begin to fill the air with singing. A red squirrel chases a gray squirrel across the street.

At the stop light, turn right. Roll south, past the college, the cemetery, the apartments, the pharmacist, the other neighborhoods, the minimalls, the veterinarian. Stop in to get some coffee, to fill the thermos as well as the mug. Stretch the legs one more time. Look around, gather the town on this one morning into a still-life memory. Then get back into the car. Roll toward the interstate highway, I-94. Begin the trip.

4

In the Middle Ages, the Western world was big enough to need a picture of itself, a *mappa mundi,* a map of the world. The question wasn't "Where are we?" The question was "How do this place, this house, this field, and this tree fit into a larger picture? I know there are things I cannot see."

"What's over there?" we mused. "What's it like?"

Beyond the known world there was only hope, and fear, and imagination. And a map provokes the wonderings of the imagination. Christian Scripture said Jerusalem was in the midst of nations, so the mapmakers put it in the center of their maps. The closer you were to Jerusalem, the closer you were to Christ. Beyond the walls of Jerusalem were the other cities and places of the then-known world. And at the end of the known world, the mapmakers drew monsters. Abarimon, with backward-turned feet. Amyctyrae, with a lower lip large enough to be used as an umbrella. Astomi, with no mouths and who lived by smell. Blemmyae, with their faces in their chests. Cynocephali, with the heads of dogs.

5

Accelerate. Merge. Join the westbound flow, the cars, the pickup and semitrailers, the men and women who are not at home but whose trips will lead them nowhere new. Exceed the speed limit. As it traverses Moorhead, Minnesota, and Fargo, North Dakota, I-94 is six lanes wide—too much space for the lightness of early morning traffic. Look around a bit more than normal. The storm cell moved out of town heading south. A small though brilliant rainbow falls away from the back edge of the cloud. The town looks washed. Leave the radio off. Listen to the sounds of tire and wind and water and road. Roll a window down, then get ready to exit. Pull to the right. Exit I-94 West and join I-29 North.

North!

North is the direction for this story.

Glance at the passenger seat, the open map resting there. Scan the roads that will lead north, west, north, west, north, north, north. North takes the car out of town, out of the county, out of the country. North will cross the Arctic Circle, in a land filled with grizzly bears and polar bears, caribou and moose, ptarmigan and gyrfalcon. North will enter a land where the people call themselves Gwich'in and Inuvialuit. If all roads begin at the end of my driveway, north leads to the farpoint, where the road finally ends, where the only tools I will have are hope and fear and imagination.

6

"You are here."

What a wonderful piece of information! Of course, this news is oftentimes depressing as I discover I'm standing in front of a mall directory, between a shoe store and a corn dog counter, but to know for just one brief moment exactly where I am is seldom less than thrilling. Science tells me that my body is spinning on the surface of this planet at nearly 1,040 miles per hour, that the planet is spinning around the sun at nearly 66,640 miles per hour, that the sun is spinning around the galaxy, that the galaxy is spinning around the universe, all of us racing away from wherever we started. Then again, Einstein tells us that speed and location are relative, given the position and speed of multiple observers, and phenomenology argues that everything I can possibly know is really just a good guess anyway. So when I am told "You are here" with a little arrow pointing to an even littler dot, I often want to sing.

There is a moment, psychologists tell us, when an infant discovers he or she is not its mother, that the infant is a separate being. And at this moment, Desire is born. Desire for the Other. D. W. Winnicott calls the imagined distance between the Self and the Other a Potential Space. Yet, there is another way to look at this moment. When an infant discovers its Self, what other question is there than "Where am I?" And, when the infant sees the mother, what other question is there than "Why aren't I over there?" If Desire is born at the moment of self-awareness, I believe it is a desire to travel.

Locating ourselves in terms of a physical geography and in relation to other people is the first human task, the first question of an infant. Certainly, "Where am I?" is also the question we ask as life slips from us and we enter whatever comes next. And perhaps this one question, in its first and final forms, in the myriad forms it takes during the course of a life, during the course of a civilization, is why we are so in love with maps, why we pause in front of them, linger over them without a prior question. A map is a promise, a pledge to pin something down just long enough to see it.

7

IN THE MIDDLE AGES, "Where am I?" or "Where are we?" found its answer less in geography than in theology, philosophy, and politics. Maps had nothing to do with finding your way. Instead, there were Noachid maps, often called T-O maps, which sprang from the post-Flood story of Noah sending his sons out to the new lands— Japheth to Europe, Shem to Asia, and Ham to Africa. T-O maps put North to the left and imagined the solid ground surrounded by ocean at every horizon. The ring of ocean formed the letter *O*. The Mediterranean was the stem of the *T*; the Tanais River and then the Nile formed the letter's top.

And there were the more theoretical Macrobian zone maps, divided into broad bands from top to bottom. The top and bottom bands were uninhabitable places because of cold. The middle band represented a place uninhabitable because of heat. The not-too-hot and not-too-cold places were "Nostra Zona," Our Zone.

These maps were popular, well known, stained on the glass of church windows and woven into tapestries. They had titles like *De Philosophia Mundi*, Concerning the Philosophy of the World, and what's more—they were pretty to see.

There is a way to ask "Where am I?" that means "How do I get to where I am not?" This need for an answer gives rise to road maps. Yet, there is a way to ask "Where am I?" that has nothing to do with leaving home. This need gives rise to *De Philosophia Mundi*.

Theoretical or theological, medieval maps had Grace in the center and monsters at the frontier. Yet, the edge is as often attractive as repellent.

8

WHAT DO YOU TAKE when you've never been to where you're going? In my office, I'd shown my route to Per Anderson, a religion professor, a friend. My finger followed the highways joining British Columbia, the Yukon, the Northwest Territories.

"You going to carry?" he asked me.

"Huh?"

"You going to take a gun?"

"A gun?"

His own finger touched the red line called the Dempster Highway.

"Scott," he said, "that's grizzly country. There are bears up there who could think of you as lunch."

"Oh," I said. Looking at the flat white map on a table in my office, I saw mountains and rivers and ways of seeing the sunlight not possible near my home. Per, looking at that same map, saw bears.

"You know," I told him later, "only a religion professor asked me if I was prepared to kill something."

"Yeah," he replied. "It's a complicated life."

9

How is it possible that strangers can understand each other, can know each other in ways more intimate and personal than lovers, than husbands and wives, than parents and children? We've all had that feeling. In the quiet of an after-midnight reading, curled up alone in a chair, on a couch or in bed, a character suddenly hits a chord in our soul. Standing in front of a painting, we see more than colors and patterns; we see the depth of a creator's ways of knowing. Listening to favorite music, the physical world supporting our feet becomes invisible, irrelevant, and language loses any application to the longings and affirmations spoken by string, by air, and by drum.

Art connects humanities. The work of the artist is the work of shouting, "Here I am! This is what I believe!" And those of us who listen come to know the worker as well as the work. I know Shakespeare, what he believed, what he felt, what he loved, and what he feared, better than I know my neighbor. And my neighbor knows Shakespeare better than she knows me. So the sensibilities of a man who died in the Renaissance continue to make Community as a third millennium begins.

Likewise, I have come to know a man named John Norden, who walked the Renaissance streets of England during the days of Shakespeare. John Norden was the queen's mapmaker. In 1593, or thereabouts, he began a survey of Britain—"not merely from business motives," according to M. St. Clare Byrne, "but prompted equally by his own real love of the countryside itself."

John Norden lived when Walter Raleigh lived, when Francis Drake lived. And while Raleigh and Drake returned with exotic stories of the world's corners, replacing the fear of monsters with a monstrous desire for gold, Norden gave light to a landscape made invisible through familiarity. It seems that he, and only he among his peers, understood not only what a map could do, but also what it could be. Again according to Byrne, "[W]ith the sole exception of

Norden the topographers were all too interested in imparting their knowledge of an England that had been, to take the time to describe for our delight the England that lay around them. . . . Here is that interest in humanity and in his own day that gives Norden his unique position."

Here, he says, is my map. Here, on his map, says the scholar, is his interest in humanity.

10

INTERSTATE 29 NORTH OUT OF FARGO. No one else in the rearview mirror or on the road still to come. The light rain is constant while downpour cells move over fields of sugar beets and grains and sunflowers like checker pieces on a gargantuan scale.

One hundred and fifteen miles north of home, I pull off at some lonely exit, pause at the top of the overpass to taste the rain and wind and temperature, the constitution of the prairie this day.

Nothing on my road map tells me the land here is different. No picture, no words, no legend tells me all water here flows north, that I am driving deeper into the bed of the Pleistocene Lake Agassiz. No markings on my road map tell me about the hundreds of intercontinental ballistic missiles now housed a stone's throw to the west. While the historical and political questions and curiosities travel with me, the historical and political and other maps—the historical and political and other answers—remain behind. This is a choice. Every answer is a partial answer, and to carry a partial answer in front of a new question in a new land is to enforce a blindness.

On the surface, the land here looks like it does at my front door. And my road map tells me this place is connected to what I know. So, in my personal map, the one etched out on the walls of my inner eye, I have a way to start. I am making my own map here, the map of my own history, my own explorations, in a limited time.

Tighten the seat belt. Go over the inventory. Jeans. Shirts. A sweatshirt. Two sweaters. Raincoat. A good pair of hiking boots. Emergency medical kit. CB radio. Stop-Leak for the radiator. Jelly beans. Hat. Fishing pole. Sunglasses. Money.

11

WITH RALEIGH AND DRAKE, Shakespeare and Norden, there were also Mercator and Ortelius. And each man shared one thing, which was not a love of place. Farmers can love a place. Tax collectors can love a place for entirely different reasons. Saints and sinners can love the same place equally. Love of place is personal, unspoken, deeper than language.

Yet, someone in the Renaissance, maybe everyone at the same time, discovered that Place also means Story, that a map is an invitation to follow a story in a global language. "Look at my map," says the farmer. "This is the story of what will grow." "Look at my map," says the tax collector. "This is the story of wealth."

Story creates Community. And someone else's Story creates Desire.

I am in love with maps. All maps. Topographical maps. Road maps. Maps that show population density, divorce rates, educational levels, habits of watching television or how many magazines are delivered per household, sociological trends. Census maps. Very old maps, showing trails long since covered or replaced or removed. Weather maps. Two- and three-dimensional maps. Campus maps. City bus route maps. Mineral maps. Maps of the ocean floor and maps of high-altitude wind patterns. Harbor maps. Shopping mall directory maps. Maps for pilots. Maps for scuba divers. Maps for fire departments.

And not only those maps that can be put on paper or a video screen. There are linguistic maps, cognitive maps, and the directions offered from local resident to tourist on the best way to get to the beach. Each morning I walk into my son's or daughter's room, and their first reaction to being awakened provides a map of that morning, whether the distance between their rooms and school will be smooth and dry and paved, or rough and graveled in a midnight windstorm. Each day, each person and each corner provide a map of what lies ahead, a promise or portent of what most likely will come.

We make our plans from the maps we are given and the maps we seek. Not only the best roadway to work or the grocery store, updated by helicopters or radio reports, but when to approach others with good or troubling news. When to tell a joke. When to shut the door and let others pass by the self-construction zones.

12

AT THE BORDER, the rainfall is briefly torrential. I wait behind a white sedan and then a motor home with Michigan license plates, each of us approaching a low brown-and-white drive-through customs station. It's midmorning now, and we all have our lights on.

We are leaving the country, entering a place more in our heads than our history. On the other side of the raised traffic island, Canadian cars enter the States. The drivers on both sides sit somehow straighter because the rules have changed.

When I get to the booth, where a uniformed man leans on one elbow out a window to talk to me, the questions are perfunctory.

"Where are you going?"

"Inuvik," I say, trying not to smile, "then Tuktoyaktuk."

Inuvik. Tuktoyaktuk. Surely, I think, these names would cause even a border guard to raise an eyebrow. These places are three thousand miles away, at the edge of the continent. It's all I can do not to reach over to the passenger seat and grab my atlas, hold it out the window for him, and point. "Here," I could say, half my finger on land, half my finger in the Arctic Ocean's Beaumont Sea. "Here! Here is where I am going!" But his questions aren't really important. Somewhere, a guard I cannot see is putting my license plate number into a computer, checking me against some list of the desperate, the wanted, and the not wanted at all. I could tell this man I was driving to Kathmandu. The permission to let me enter a new country will come from someone and something else.

"Do you have any pets with you?"

"No."

"Do you have any weapons?"

"Just my fishing rod."

This gets a smile. "Go on," he says. "Don't forget to buy a license."

A short distance north of the border, with a large parking lot, canary-yellow walls, red doorway arches, banners and flags and an immaculate lawn, the Travel Manitoba Visitors' Center waits for people with questions. But I am stopped at the door by two signs on white paper. Large red block letters at the bottom of each page read "Tourist Alert," and there is an exclamation mark running the entire height of the page.

"JOHN & DOREEN SEMKO, of Wadena, SK—traveling through Southern Can. or Northern USA from Yellowstone National Park to Brandon, MB. PLEASE CONTACT BARBARA SEMKO." And then two phone numbers.

"MR. FREDIRICH AUBREY HELD from Goldlake, Alberta—traveling to Maine, USA in a white 1985 Ezlo trailer pulling a 1989 Yellow Jeep. PLEASE CONTACT ANNE GREGORY IN MAINE." And then just one phone number.

It is impossible to know if these signs imply disaster or simply a change of plans. And it is impossible not to imagine Barbara Semko and Anne Gregory, whoever they are, standing with a cup of coffee over some map of their own, wondering, "Where are they?"

Inside the welcome center, enthusiastic women offer currency exchange and information. Brochures and maps fill an entire wall. I ask about John and Doreen Semko, about Mr. Fredirich Aubrey Held, but the women shake their heads. "We just put up the signs," one of them says.

"Don't you ever want to call those phone numbers, just to see how things turned out?" I ask.

"No," the women say. "We put up too many of those."

Get back in the car. Drive north.

13

EVERYTHING, IT SEEMS, is mappable. And we have the desire to map, it seems, everything.

Like all people, I need to know where I am. Physically. Morally. Intellectually. Historically. To know where I am, I need to know my place in a larger world. Maps detail the world for me. A red sign on a directory tells me "You are here" and points to a corner by a coffee shop. The body language of my colleagues says "You are here" and points to a corner in their day. A book in my office maps the migratory patterns of birds found in Minnesota. A textbook on logic maps how conclusions are made. Books map the nervous system, the history of the Grand Canyon wall, the physical causes of romantic love, the hierarchy of Heaven. Maps give me a set of choices to make, a set of possible pathways.

All people share curiosity. No matter how far apart we may be in terms of gender, class, race, geophysical locale, we all have a love of Story, which is a love of the forecast. What will happen next? Which road will be taken? And for the forecast to mean anything, we have to know what's at risk—how the past has led to the moment, now, we are looking forward. In every culture since the beginning of time, storytellers have been the elite. Storytellers are the actors, the authors, the anchors on the evening news, the comedians, the friend down the hall who's heard a good one. Storytellers lay out the map of the past and the map of what is still possible.

Storytellers and maps tell us what might happen. But sometimes they are wrong.

14

MY FRIEND John Wheeler is a storyteller, a mapmaker, a weatherman. He's one of the men and women who fill that midsection of our local evening news to tell the ongoing story of what will move from heaven to earth, the wind and rain and hail and bright summer sunshine. Our lives often depend on them.

Each evening they put maps on the television screen that we read much the same way we read detective stories. The pressure map details the location and strength of the approaching front. What will happen? Will it flatten the local crops with hail? Will that storm we see on the radar map spawn a tornado? Will I need a parka, a raincoat, boots?

Each evening the story ends with a cliffhanger, an ellipsis, a set of possibilities, a promise of more maps tomorrow.

John's office is set just to the side of the stage used for broadcast. One wall is covered with North American and world maps: Surface Analysis; 850 Millibar Analysis; 700, 500, 300, and 200 Millibar Analysis. A computer model map is called the MRF map, the medium-range forecast. There are the NGM, or Nested Grid models, and the new ETA models. The other walls hold books on physics and chaos theory, computer screens and keyboards and light-pen panels. One side is open toward the stage.

We are talking about the weather I will find on my trip, and John tells me it should be fine. He's been to the Arctic himself, following polar bears near Churchill. He calls up the current temperature for Inuvik on a computer, and it's seventy-five degrees Fahrenheit. "You know what that means, don't you?" he asks me. "It means you'll be breathing mosquitoes."

I ask John where the maps he gives to us come from. The satellite pictures and local radar come from NOAA, he says. The national radar comes from a company in Boston that collects all the local readings and makes a composite.

The picture of the country placed underneath the radar and satellite images is satellite photography; the boundaries of states are on a map drawn by the Central Intelligence Agency. "We have geographic data for the United States," John tells me, "but not for Canada or Mexico."

"John," I say, pointing to a television screen showing the underlay picture, "then why do I see mountains here, in Canada and Mexico?"

"My computer has a paintbox program," he says. "I made those mountains."

With a light pen, John draws a frontal boundary over and along a series of pressure lines.

"How many maps do you put up in the course of a three-and-a-half-minute report?" I ask.

"That depends on how you're counting," he says. "Each animation is really a collection of seventy or eighty still-picture maps. But if you count each animation as one, then I put up about ten or eleven different maps, not counting other graphics."

"How many maps go into the making of those maps?"

"In the course of a day, I scan about one hundred and fifty new maps."

"And how many acts of interpretation are involved with those hundred and fifty?"

"Thousands," he says. "Maybe even tens of thousands—all of it based on experience. See the local radar over there? See that big wedge-shaped blank thing heading northeast? We have no image for that area right now. I don't know why. But that doesn't mean that part of the universe has suddenly disappeared. All over the world, small and large corrections are made all the time. We always put what we see with what we know. Let me give you another example. When they were first put together, the computer models of weather coming over the Cascade mountains never worked the way the weather did. The problem was the height of the mountains. The only way they could get the model to work right was to move the mountains, make them broad instead of tall. In that model, the mountains extend miles out into what is really the Pacific Ocean—but it gives us an accurate picture of the weather."

John's business is mapmaking. He has maps on his walls, in his computers, and in his head.

"Out of all this," I ask, "what's most important?"

"The words," he says. "The story is what people listen to."

15

WEST OF SASKATOON, a broad bright-green-and-yellow valley appears on the northern side of the Yellowhead. The prairie swells every other direction. A small gravel rest stop allows drivers to take in the view. For humans, seeing any distance at all is always a cause for pleasure.

An interpretive sign offers a map and explanation of the migrations of whooping cranes:

> Saskatchewan serves as an important feeding and migration area for the graceful and endangered whooping crane. It is fascinating to see a whooping crane flying overhead with its neck and legs fully extended. Spiraling upward on warm air currents then gliding towards its destination on its migratory path through Saskatchewan (shown on map), the whooping crane relies on Saskatchewan's marshes, shallow creeks and agricultural land as its source of food.

Another sign maps the story of the Doukhobors. "In 1899, a group of Doukhobors from Russia established the first village of Kirilovka one half mile west of here. . . . [T]hese settlers, seeking religious freedom, thrived despite severe hardships, deprivations and cold."

In the valley, the North Saskatchewan River glides by a railroad line. Overhead, the sky is clear and sunny.

How many maps are possible? How many questions can be asked about any one small individual spot on this planet? If I ask, "Where am I?" how many different versions of "You are here" are possible?

Standing at the edge of the river valley, I know I am in the middle of a map of bird migrations, standing in a map of human migration as well. I know the rail company has a map of its tracks, as the highway department has its own maps of this road, detailing not only where it goes but also its repairs and future. I can assume there are mineral maps of this valley, questions about oil or rock. I can assume there are topographical maps, and hunting maps, and census maps.

But as I type these sentences about that valley, I am in my office. The number *308* is on the wall outside my office door, which locates me in the progression of numbers in this third-floor hallway. Somewhere, there is a set of plans or blueprints that shows my office in relation to the others on this floor, to the others in this building, to the pipes and wires and windows and doors and fire escapes and closets that make up the possible transit choices in what is collectively called Academy Hall. Academy Hall is located in relation to the other buildings on the campus directory, which is printed on paper for the visitors who make it to the campus information office, as well as set in stone and concrete near the main parking lot. And if I let the circle grow, the number of maps explodes.

So, where am I? I am in the psychological map of ascending or descending office numbers students and others carry in their heads. I am in a set of building plans (and, actually, several differing versions and sets of these plans, as plans are also drawn to predict or answer fairly specific needs—Where is that pipe? You want a telephone line put where?). I am on the campus maps. I am near the North Saskatchewan River, a few hundred feet above and south of the waterway. I am in a place where whooping cranes feed and Doukhobors settled. And, I am in your head, dear reader, wherever you may be right now.

Can any map say, "You Are Here," and get it right?

16

MAPS DO NOT COME FROM GOD. And, according to Mark Monmonier, distinguished professor of geography at Syracuse University,

> Not only is it easy to lie with maps, it's essential. To portray meaningful relationships for a complex, three-dimensional world on a flat sheet of paper or a video screen, a map must distort reality. As a scale model, the map must use symbols

that almost always are proportionally much bigger or thicker than the features they represent. To avoid hiding critical information in a fog of detail, the map must offer a selective, incomplete view of reality. There's no escape from the cartographic paradox: to present a useful and truthful picture, an accurate map must tell white lies.

Little comfort as the rain returns, a storm cell strong enough I will hear about it again tomorrow morning, in a hotel room, watching CNN. How far to Edmonton? The map said nothing about the oil refinery at the Saskatchewan-Alberta border. The map said nothing about the change from canola and grain to pine forest. The map said nothing about gigantic buffalo feeding near the fence line.

Trace the map lines with a finger, try to judge distance, equate distance with time. Compute the gas mileage and the need for sleep.

17

DRIVE WEST into the deepening evening light. The Yellowhead Route into Edmonton. Signs on lampposts and billboards give the details too fine for a road atlas. Turn off at this exit. Turn right at this street. The world's largest shopping mall is here, with sharks and dolphins, water slides and more submarines than the Canadian navy, with a roller coaster that has killed and a hotel named Fantasyland.

Trust your sense of direction as well as your sense of self. Look for all the signs that say, "You Are Here."

AN ADVENT NATURE

1. Summer Solstice: The Straight River

I CANNOT TELL YOU HOW LONG THE FOX HAD BEEN DEAD. AND I cannot tell you how it died. My morning had been filled already with enough stories of the living to carry me home. Stories of brown trout that did, or more often did not, take to the small flies I was dropping in front of them as I stood in the middle of the Straight River, northern Minnesota. Stories of egrets, geese, red-winged blackbirds, pelicans, sparrows, and robins. Stories of bugs. Stories of the flatland prairie near my home, cultivated fields of grains and sugar beets, giving way to hills and clear lakes, forests of birch, pine, oak, and elm as I drove east. Stories of an early morning thunderstorm giving way to a crimson sunrise. A story about something very large moving through the river behind me, far enough around a bend in the river I could not see it, but not so far away I could not imagine its size from the sound it made. Imagined stories of moose, bear, timber wolf, deer.

It had been a daybreak with theater, with symphony, with thunderbolts and fast river water, with fish leaping and birds diving. So much motion on what most people would call a quiet morning.

I am lucky to have seen the fox at all. I had stopped to fill a pipe, not unhappily offering some tobacco to the river in the process, and for some time just stood there feeling the water whirl its way around my waders. The thunderstorms were leaving, heading east, and the wind was lessening. The trees, the grasses, the world were glimmering. I wasn't really thinking about anything, I suppose. Just looking. More than once I forgot the fishing, happy just to be a witness.

All I noticed at first were two ears sticking up from a reddish mat nestled in the crook of a fallen tree. I walked a little closer and still did not know what I was seeing. Only when I'd come around and could see it head-on did I make sense of the shape.

There is a part of me that would like to imagine this fox had a choice, that it somehow knew its time had come and that it picked this particular set of branches as the best place to discover whatever comes next for foxes. Its nose pointed west, toward where the sun sets at this time of the summer. And in northern Minnesota, midsummer twilight lasts for hours. It could have been a leave-taking filled with happy retrospect and quiet anticipation. But even I know better than this.

I sat on a stump in the river and looked at this fox. Nothing in this morning suggested death, but here it was. Not eloquent or filled with metaphor, but elegant and sacred. There was no larger symbol here, no sadness or sense of loss. The death of a north-woods fox causes nothing. But for me, this fox completed the picture. The morning had been alive with sky and river and animals, easily taken in. This fox was evidence that the story of this river, this place, is larger than I will ever see.

"Amen," I said to the fox. Not as benediction. But as confirmation.

2. 308 Academy Hall

I WILL NEVER CLIMB EVEREST. This much is already certain. In all probability, I will never hike the length of the Grand Canyon. I will not likely spend a season at the South Pole, although I'd like to, and I'll never get a chance to walk unhurriedly through the Amazon basin or the Chinese highlands.

Most days I walk the hundred yards or so from my home to my office, amble a bit from office to classroom and back, then walk the hundred yards back to my home. But those other places, those places I have not seen and will never see, those places I can only imagine, are not less real to me, nor less sacred. Maps and pictures of those places hang on my walls; journals and texts fill my bookshelves. The untraveled road has always been the one most anticipated, the one most imagined, the one whose promise we most desire.

I've had good fortune. I've traveled already more than most people ever will. And for me, the act of traveling, the act of encountering each new corner of the natural world, is bound to the idea of Advent. Advent is a season of preparation, of housecleaning, of getting ready for the miraculous. It's a season of joy-filled anticipation. We know what's coming. At least we know the mundane elements, since we've done the routine before. But even with this knowing, the excitement builds. All through Advent, we make ourselves ready, get ourselves looking in a direction we too often ignore.

I think there is something essential in the idea of Advent, something we feel more deeply important than we've explained to ourselves. And the same is true for how we see nature. We live in our cities and towns, most of us, but we are constantly anticipating what exists outside the people-made places. I will never be most places on the planet, but I anticipate them every day.

Friends who are religion professors tell me that in Advent we are in fact getting ready for three Christmases. The first is the historical Christmas. The second is the metaphorical, present-day Christmas. And the third is the Christmas of the Second Coming. The Kingdom of Heaven will not replace this world, the one we're living in. This world will become that kingdom. Martin Luther made the point sometimes that we should stop saying God created the world, and instead speak in the present tense, that God is creating this world.

And this is troubling news. If I am going to claim we have an Advent relationship with the natural world, with both wildness and wilderness, then I am claiming a relationship with a historic Nature, which is troubling because we've romanticized it so much. And with a present-day Nature, which is troubling because no one disagrees about its metaphorical power—look at all the nature shows on television and the sheer weight of old *National Geographic* magazines filling our basements—yet we can cut down forests so easily as well. And with a future Nature, which is troubling because simple population pressure seems to be the death knell of any open places. Still, despite the trouble, in an Advent relation with Nature, we are anticipating the very thing that can save us. All three relations are, in fact, calls to action.

Advent is a time to cleanse the imagination, to see the world sacramentally once again. Advent anticipates Christmas, divinity made real in the world, while in Nature there is simply the fragile promise of otherness. It could be that these two things are in fact the same.

3. *Uluru*

"Nganana Tatintja Wiya" means "We do not climb."
It's all over the tourist brochures.

> "What visitors call the climb is the traditional route taken
> by ancestral Mala men on their arrival at Uluru and the path is
> of spiritual significance. Although permission for climbing is
> given, the traditional owners, Anangu, prefer that you choose
> to respect the cultural significance of Uluru and do not climb."

Standing at the base of Uluru, what most people call Ayers Rock, in the central outback of Australia, I'm caught by the sight of people all over the rock. Tourists, by carload and busload, pull into the car park and usually without hesitation race toward the climb. There's a line of people going up, and another line coming down. In a brochure I learn that Anangu call tourists *Minga,* which means ants.

"Did you climb?" I ask a young man sitting on a bench.

"Yes," he said.

"What do you think of the request not to climb?"

"Well, at first I thought about that. I mean, I suppose it's a bit like crawling all over a crucifix in a church."

"But you made the climb."

"Yes, I did. I finally decided to, since I'll probably never be here again."

Turning away, I begin what is called the Mala walk, a portion of the base of the rock, interpretive brochure in hand.

Life and Land are One

The Tjukurpa is not a dream; it is real. The landscape tells how the knowledge and wisdom of our ancestors came to be. The land was made at the beginning of the Tjukurpa, when ancestral beings created the landscape features and all living creatures including humans. The details of the activities and travels of the ancestral beings have been taught to us ever since, in story, song, dance and ceremony. When Anangu look at the land, and all the features and living things upon it, we see visible evidence that our ancestral beings still exist. Uluru, and its many different features, continue to tell us about the Tjukurpa. We have no need for special buildings to remind us of our religion or Law. The Tjukurpa is all around us in the landscape itself.

I continue the Mala walk, reading about the Mala people coming to Uluru from the West and North, about how they would plant a *Ngaltawata,* a ceremonial pole, on top of the rock, which would signal that everything to follow would be ceremony. I read how other people came from the West and about the fatal disagreements that would follow. I pass the sites of this story, the story itself made manifest in the rock and caves and water holes.

At a cave called Mala Puta, I catch up with a park ranger giving a tour to about fifty people. In the brochure I read that "Anangu believe that a site such as Mala Puta is too important to have its relationship with all the surrounding land ignored, removed and isolated in a photograph." The ranger repeats the same request. Mala Puta, spiritually, is the pouch of the female hare-wallaby.

The ranger and the group move on, but two men linger. When the group has gone beyond eyesight, they quickly shoot several pictures.

4. 308 Academy Hall

THIS MUCH IS CERTAIN. We have grown accustomed in stories to the sight of a wise man on a mountaintop. It seems perfectly reasonable for him to be there. Away from the noise of humanity, he can gain the ability to listen and the time to think. And we are no longer surprised by the location of monasteries in difficult and remote landscapes, for the very same reason.

In the fourth century, the Desert Fathers took to the desert to discover more clearly what they meant by God. Only by shedding what they called their passions, their connections to the issues and politics of their daily lives, could they approach an appreciation of the physical world; and only from this appreciation could they approach theology.

The solitary spiritual quest in the wilderness is not limited to any cultural tradition. It is shared by Native Americans, Buddhists, Inuit, and Boy Scouts. If there is one thing we know as a species, it is that we must maintain our connections, and our participations, in a world that moves before politics and doctrine. We know this, and it scares us.

The Greeks defined themselves by membership in the city-state. If you were not a member, that is, if you came from the wilderness, you were often the enemy. And nature itself was often the enemy. The city-state was order and rule and status quo, while nature, both literally and metaphorically, was random, hard, lethal, by definition uncivil. From the time the first hut was erected to this very day, we have been working to divorce ourselves from the threat of nature.

Still, the stories work the other way. The desert did not kill Moses, or Jesus. It made them stronger. John the Baptist was the voice in the wilderness. For Christians, Advent readings begin with the Kingdom of God becoming the highest peak on Earth, and from the mountain comes the news to turn sword into plowshare. Advent readings show John submerging Jesus in the river, and only then does a voice from Heaven proclaim his readiness. If we have an Advent relation with the natural world, then we are aware, dimly, that the stories are not over, that the threat still exists, and that the threat itself is what may save us. "In Wildness," said Thoreau, "is the preservation of the world."

What do we seek in Nature? We seek what we fear, which is confirmation that we are incomplete.

5. Mount Cook

NOTHING IS MORE DIFFICULT to escape than our own stories. In Minnesota, when I speak the word *home,* what I really mean is everything from Medora and the Badlands of North Dakota to the St. Croix River at the Wisconsin border. This is the part of the world where I am most often. Between those two boundaries, I have stories, stories I've learned from other people and stories I've helped create myself. And every story has its own setting, its own landscape and earth.

The closer I get to home, the more stories I have. Prairie land just east of home is not just prairie, it's the spot where I sat one morning in a blind with two others, watching and listening to the mating dance and song of prairie chickens. North of town is the spot I stopped to rest from too much driving and discovered a moose in some trees not twenty yards away. When I pass these places now, those stories insist themselves back into the present tense.

Usually, this insistence is a wonderful thing. Few things are more welcome among people than a good story, and good stories shared with others are what create friendships, communities, security, and love. But there are those other places where we have no personal history, no personal or community story to color the landscape for us in advance. And it's in those other places that we can regain a sense of the wild.

This particular morning, I am sitting on a rock on a trail that leads to Kea Point, in the shadow of Mount Cook, in the Otago region of the south island of New Zealand. Mount Cook is the country's highest peak, permanently snowcapped, and this morning quite breathtaking set against a deep-blue sky, set on fire by the sunshine. The trail has led me through river washes, through dense brush, over small hills, and up steep climbs. Not one step puts me anyplace I've been before, or anyplace the people I know have been before. For me, this morning, this is a landscape without human story, without interpretation, without metaphor or politics. Keas, a type of alpine parrot, fly overhead while glacier runoff wets my boots.

When I am at home, my sense of where I am holds years of history, years of community and people and politics and the thousand concerns of a social life. Here, looking up at a mountain I've never seen before this morning, my sense of where I am holds nothing more than rock, than water, than birds and trees and bush. Here, apart from the insistence of others, I am able to catch a breath of the Other. There is no past in this place today, and no future. Just a tremendous present-filling eternity. It's enough to fill the soul.

There are places on this planet that are sacred to me. Not because they have been sanctified by ritual, but because they have not.

6. *Wright Pass*

A SACRED PLACE CAN TROUBLE as well as bring joy. In fact, trouble may be as necessary for the sacred as a fall is for salvation.

A fair distance north of the Arctic Circle, almost exactly upon a continental divide, at a place called Wright Pass, I am marveling at the bright midsummer sun, despite the fact it's well past midnight.

This same sunshine, I realize, also falls on London, on Moscow, on Delhi and Johannesburg now, and the sentimental part of my nature wants to cry out in this new connection with what I consider the other side of the planet. I am sharing something as simple and as physical and as joy-giving as sunshine on my face with places and people I'll never know. Right now, looking up from this mountain pass, with no other human within any reasonable distance, it's possible to imagine the size of the globe.

"Hello!" I yell northward.

Then, of course, I remember that my own home is in darkness now. Every step toward a new place takes us away from someplace we know. The wind at Wright Pass is strong, and I decide silence and reverence are the better ways of seeing this place. Brilliant red fireweed, the greens and browns of Arctic tundra grasses and willows, the patches of snow still in the mountains have their own stories to tell.

I am at Wright Pass this night because of something called the Dempster Highway. More than four hundred miles of single-lane gravel each way from Dawson City in the Yukon Territory to Inuvik in the Northwest Territories, it's the only public road in North America to cross the Arctic Circle. The fact that this road exists is what has brought me here, the strong call of a simple line on a map leading toward the imagined places. And the fact that this road exists is what troubles the picture for me.

Looking southward from the pass, I can see the landscape fall away toward a brown valley, then rise again into another range of mountains. And in the middle of the scene, the dark line of the road. It doesn't matter how long or where I look here, my eye is always drawn back to the roadway, to the very thing that connects me to a world I've been leaving. The Dempster Highway connects me, yes, with people I know and love. And it has brought me to ptarmigan and grizzly bear and views large enough to steal my breath. At the same time it connects me with other things, with my need for gasoline, with politics, with the million messy ways we've arranged ourselves, with money and greed and division.

To be at Wright Pass is to be in a privileged place. Here, and at other places like here, if we listen, we can begin to hear the sounds outside the insistence of humanity. Voices much older than our own. Voices we have a talent to forget. Voices we must not ever forget.

Yet, if I am able to hear or see anything here, if I am able to expand even for a moment my understanding of the natural world, the cost of my new understanding is several hundred miles of road interrupting what I've come to see. Anticipating the Other, I have come to Wright Pass. Anticipating me, other people have built roads, gas stations, hotels, restaurants, gift shops.

I resist turning nature into symbol or metaphor, to give it a meaning-made-human. The grizzly bear that lumbered away from me earlier today does not care how or why I was looking at it. But the road is a different matter. The road is a symbol of commerce, of ease, of accessibility. Yes, I am grateful for this road. And yes, I worry about how many others will come after me. I admit to this selfishness. But today I traveled several hundred miles of Arctic landscape at more than fifty miles per hour.

At Wright Pass I catch a moment of illumination. And to get here, I committed a sin.

7. Sixth Street

I USED TO LIVE IN AN OLD HOUSE.

Built in 1929, it was filled with oak floors, heavy ceiling moldings and window frames, lathe and plaster walls that cracked anew every season, and the accumulated story-ghosts of every love and heart broken within its history. Like many old homes, nothing really fit anymore. The doors caught on their frames. The windows took some effort to convince. Every step on the staircase had claimed its particular note in the scales of squeaks and wheezes. If you sat very still in the living room, you could feel the footfalls of the others in the house come through the walls, the floor, up into the upholstery of the couch. I believe there's no other way to say it: old houses dance.

Still, old houses are not easy places. Entropy and the weight of Minnesota snowfalls had worked their way into the wood that supports a small deck off the second floor and into the spaces between the cinder blocks that make up the foundation. Each season the house shifted a little more, and new cracks appeared in some wall. I cannot imagine a time anywhere in the future when that house, or any house, will not ask for some repair, for some help, for some participation, for some small act of protection and love.

I loved this house, not in spite of its creaks but in part because of them. That house, like our new one now, sheltered me and my family from rain and snow, from heat and lethal cold, but only if we sheltered the house from decay, from time and neglect and stupidity. It's a relationship in which we both must take an active and loving part. The rewards are substantial.

Not so very long ago, one twilight found neighbors and friends gathered in the backyard. Kids ran and played. Dogs barked and jumped. Long after the coals in the grill had gone to deep red and then ashen embers, the grown-ups fell quiet. From where we sat, we could see the many homes on that shaded street. We could see, in the failing light, visible proof of a very small planet's rotation through space. We could see the never-ending game of tag turned into hide-and-seek turned back into tag. Past, present, future.

Somehow, for all of us at the same moment, there was a moment of clarity. A moment of connectedness. A moment when we could glimpse the promise that the universe and all its places will continue not despite or because of us, but simply with us. In the deepening blues of the evening sky, in the games of the children, in the comfortable silences of adults who have become friends, there were hints of the sacred. Yes, there is no other way to say it. We could see, we could almost touch and taste, the dance of time. Then one of the children ran up to her father.

"Daddy," she pleaded, "can I have some more?"

The grown-ups, feeling suddenly very young, exploded into laughter.

There are stories here, like this one, I know. Stories that are, in one sense, chapters in my own history and the history of the people I love. And there are stories about that house I will never know beyond an imagined echo from people I will never meet. Other people have patched walls here, have braced a basement wall here, have planted gardens, have laughed and loved and cried here too. And all of us have been writing the story of the future.

This, I believe, is what we mean by a sacred place. A place where the stories get large. A place where our own story meets, and joins, the stories of other people, other animals, other needs, others.

DEPARTURES

Fargo, North Dakota, is cloudy today. The type of weather most people would call miserable, lousy, hard. The clouds are low and steel gray. The water coming out of the sky is as often rain as snow, as often sideways as straight up and down.

Outside the terminal at Hector International Airport, a modern gray building that exposes its trusses and girders, orange wind socks are firmly horizontal and the flags are straight and snapping. The people walking from parking lot to terminal hold their collars close. The temperature has yet to hit forty degrees.

For Fargo, in May, this is almost cold.

Some years ago I would have thought this type of weather was a nuisance, a bother, a mess to my daily habits and routine. But I've come to know something different. In this context, this weather is precisely what we want. Farmers are smiling today because, as we close the first week in May, water is what they need most. The snowmelt has only partially readied the soil for planting. Snow, rain, any water going from sky to earth, is a promise fulfilled.

And it's difficult for me, on days like this, to imagine living anywhere other than this prairie. Not everyone in Fargo is a farmer, but none of us are very far from needing soil. People here look to the earth. We're all waiting for the crops to grow, the summer to begin, the boating season on the lakes to start, the fishing season to open. We're waiting for the things that make prairie life unfold, things that let us seek out neighbors and friends more easily.

During the rest of the year, life around here tends to be a hazard. There's nothing, literally nothing, between where we are and the North Pole. The wind that begins there comes here without a hill, without a mountain, with nothing more than a couple of trees and towns like Winnipeg to impede its progress. Windchill here can tease ninety degrees below zero; the honest temperature can pass forty below. And while some people, myself among them, find as much to love and share in the deep-cold winter, days of sun dogs and ice crystal air, springtime here like springtime everywhere is a time for breathing deeper, a time for letting things out, for letting air and sunlight and even rain in. A prairie summertime defines a type of happiness most people share.

But this morning, as I hand my ticket and passport to the ticket agent, I am leaving Fargo. This morning I am flying from Fargo to Sioux Falls, from Sioux Falls to Denver, from Denver to San Francisco, from San Francisco out over the Pacific to Honolulu, where I'll spend forty-five minutes before flying south, across the equator, across the international date line, into a different hemisphere. I am going to fly from the northern hemisphere to the southern, from the western to the eastern, from nighttime constellations I've seen since I was born to constellations I've only imagined, from heartland America to New Zealand.

New Zealand. *Te Aotearoa.* The Land of the Long White Cloud. A place more foreign to people in Fargo than Siberia. We imagine Siberia: the cold, the frigidity, the incessant hardship of living through the winter and windchill, the isolation from almost everything. It almost sounds like home. But New Zealand is one of those places that simply doesn't enter the prairie imagination. New Zealand is there, certainly. We've heard the words before. We can buy kiwifruit in our stores. We can buy some Braeburn apples as well. But the country and culture are a part of the Other. It's part of that world we know intellectually—but it remains an abstract.

When I was a child and first had a subscription to *National Geographic,* I learned to love the inaccessible places on our planet: the North and South Poles, Antarctica in general, the Himalayas, the highlands of China, the Shetland Islands, Tierra del Fuego, Everest and K2, the Outer Hebrides, Ellesmere Island. And, of course, I fell in love with New Zealand. It seemed perfect to me. A place far away. A place so far away from everything else it had no choice but social and personal self-reliance. A place I could, given enough time, come to know some of the real things about myself and my neighbors.

I've traveled before, the way most Americans have traveled. I've been to New York, Chicago, Miami. I've been to the big cities and to the holiday beaches. I've traveled around my own county, poking in at small towns to figure out why people live where they do. I've spent what has seemed like years on the interstate highways, driving to my parents' farm in Virginia, to my sister's house in Missouri, to meetings in Minneapolis or Denver. And I've been to Europe. I've visited the places of my family's origins in Denmark. I've seen London and the English countryside. I've driven the shores of Lake Geneva. I've stood at the top of the cliffs of Moher. I have had the opportunity to walk with people I consider foreign as they move through their own days in their own settings and contexts. Yet even now, even the beneficiary of such good fortune, I find it difficult to imagine New Zealand.

What I know about New Zealand I know from magazines, I know from news reports, I know from following organizations such as Greenpeace. I know they speak English in New Zealand, and Maori. I know the Moriori people came before the Maori, who came before the Europeans. I know Abel Tasman saw the islands in 1642 and named them after a province in the Netherlands. I know there are roughly three million citizens, and sixty-five million sheep. I know New Zealand was the first country on the planet to let women vote. I know they claim to have beaten the Wright brothers into the air. And I know the country is nuclear free with a passion.

What I know about New Zealand is nothing. When someone in Wellington or Auckland or Christchurch walks down the street, do they not make eye contact on purpose, like a New Yorker? Are they more congenial? Are they generally happy with or skeptical of their government? Are they generally happy with or dismayed by their lives? Are they ironic, honest, afraid? Are they lonely down there, so far away from London, Moscow, New York City? Or are they ecstatic? When the sunlight hits the ocean there, or the mountains there, how does that sunlight feel?

This trip will take me there. This trip will let me learn what it is to live, for a short while at least, in New Zealand. To look up in the nighttime sky and see the Southern Cross instead of the Big and Little Dippers. To be so far away from everything that people must rely upon their own ingenuity, their own sense of destiny and purpose and context in this universe.

I am going to New Zealand for the best of all reasons: because it's simply so far away from where I am.

But the *where I am* is no simple thing, no easy definition. This morning in Fargo the weather is not miserable. I had to live here for a while before I understood that. I needed to learn how to look at the weather with a prairie farmer's eyes, or with the eyes of the banker who has loaned money to the farmer, or with the eyes of the car dealer who wants the farmer to make money, or with the eyes of the school board who wants the tax base to grow, or with the eyes of the housing contractor who wants more people to do well, so more people move in. The people who would look at our weather today—our rain mixed with snow, our cold, our wind that seems to come stronger than the wind anywhere else in the world—and say it's miserable are looking at the weather from some other nonlocal context, some nonlocal bias. They don't understand that people here smile at springtime rain, that people here smile broadly at springtime rain that is long and consistent and stretches over weeks.

I am certain my biases will travel with me today: my desires, my hopes, my way of ordering, assimilating, constructing the universe, my way of looking at the weather. My biases are a part of my own definition, my personality, my center. They hold my love of driving on empty highways, my dislike of atonal symphonies, my joy with a good bowl of ice cream, my fear of the American Kennel Club, my pleasure near pools and lakes and rivers. And yet those biases will offer me the most trouble. They don't change easily, despite my desires.

To travel is to first leave home. Departures precede arrivals, and both deserve attention. This is as true for learning as it is location. There's nothing more challenging than to put yourself out of context. To look at others and then to look at yourself through their point of view. When I was in high school, for example, I read an account of the American War of Independence written from the British point of view. Suddenly, George Washington and Thomas Jefferson and the American patriots were no longer the anointed saints I'd been taught to believe. They were rebels, they were terrorists, they were disrupting the natural order of union. And I was no longer sure which version was right, which version of the same story held truth.

My biases will make me a tourist. They will provide the unavoidable context, the inescapable foundation of memories and values, which will leap into the middle of every sight and conversation. I hope there is a way, if I keep my eyes open enough and my mouth shut enough, I can take something of local understanding into me. I hope I can just begin to see what a New Zealander might see, just begin to hear the echoes they might hear behind a newspaper story, just begin to taste the ideas that flow backward from buying a piece of fruit. My biases will get in the way, certainly, loudly and quietly. But I've asked them to wait, be patient. We're on an adventure.

Isn't that why we travel? To place what we know up against something new and see how we fare? If I know every departure is incomplete, and every arrival is limited, isn't the new middle ground the only space I can claim as my own?

⤸

OUR PLANE THIS FIRST LEG is a common 727, mostly full. The routine of ticketing, waiting, boarding, waiting, taxiing, and then taking off is wonderful in its nonevents. When we leave Fargo, climbing over and through the clouds, rain and snow give way to bumpy weather, then brilliant sunshine over cloud patches. This is a short hop. The flight attendants have barely enough time for soda and peanuts before we're getting instructions for landing. When we come down in Sioux Falls it's partly sunny, the decisive flatness of the prairie having given way to the incessant flatness of the prairie. Even here the wind socks are flat-out horizontal to the ground. Thirty-five minutes on the ground in Sioux Falls, good humor in the plane, and then it's off again.

There is to the left of me on this flight a small woman who's terrified of flying. Every few minutes her hands go white-knuckled when she grasps the armrest between us. Every few minutes, at a particularly nasty bump in the ride, she grabs my leg and apologizes, then sits quietly in fear. The captain has provided air traffic control on one of the stereo channels, and she never takes her headset off, waiting, I suppose, for confirmation of disaster.

Softly, we land in Denver. We get out, look around—I board another plane. These departure gates look like every other gate everywhere, and I don't have time to leave the concourse. I could be anywhere.

As we're leaving Denver, the sky is beginning toward dusk. The sun is not down, but it is certainly disappearing. We climb through twenty-eight thousand feet, and the captain comes on the intercom to tell us we'll be cruising at thirty-five thousand feet, to tell us that the sky in San Francisco is sunny, although there are strong surface winds gusting to thirty-eight mph, to tell us that our views of the mountains below us should be quite wonderful. I'm sitting in the middle of row 20. To both my right and my left, young women plug in their Walkman headsets, disconnect themselves from the present tense. The woman to my left reads a romance novel titled *Sweet Memories*.

Already time has become confusing. Back in Fargo it is 7:25 in the evening. Families are just finishing dinner. I imagine my wife, Maureen, has finished feeding our daughter, Kate, and son, Andrew, who are now being hustled toward bath and bed and old stories told again. Here in Denver it is only 6:25. Dinners are just being cooked. And in San Francisco, where we're going, it is only 5:25. People aren't even home from work yet. We are chasing a sunset we're sure to lose, and each hour that direction is an hour we've somehow lost as well. It would be nice if we could relive the hours that change. We could take off at six, land at four, and then wait for that same six o'clock to come caterwauling toward us again. But I'll not get to live it over on this trip because the date line is also coming, and when we get there, I'll miss Tuesday—it simply won't exist. So this 7:25 in the evening is both Monday and Tuesday for me. This dinner is both dinners.

Most of us who fly have a vague awareness that we travel in time as well as space, but we don't talk about it. On this flight, it would be easy to argue that time travel is easier and more common than distance travel. Ten or so nearby people have headsets on, listening to music recorded sometime else. Other people are reading words written sometime else. The airplane music system offers live performances by Count Basie, Ella Fitzgerald, others who in real time are dead. Almost no one (except the flight crew, I hope) is paying much attention to the apparent *now*. In the aisles, the flight attendants are preparing dinner—meals made by someone we don't know at some other time. Underneath us fall away the centuries of the Rocky Mountains.

We've made this planet small, I think. We've made our planet one type of efficient. And in terms of air travel, at least commercial air travel in the United States, we've made our planet boring.

At just over midnight Fargo time, a 747 leaves San Francisco. We come up through some shore clouds and fog, see city lights for just a moment—the bridge and the water and everything reflected—and then we're out over the Pacific Ocean. Under way.

JUST A FEW MINUTES AWAY from land and everything has gone black outside my window. The water, the sky, the air, the clouds, the moon and stars, the cosmos—it's all simple blackness. This plane is whispering or screaming, I'm not sure which, through a void. Only the sound of the four jet engines reveals us to outside ears. Only this sound and the million electronic communications coming and going from jet to land, from jet to some outer-space satellite. Physically, we're a Doppler shot soon gone. Electronically, the world knows where we are. In a way it's spooky.

When I was living in New England, surrounded by the Berkshire Hills, we accused midwesterners of provincialism. I didn't say much, being a Missouri kid by birth, but I didn't defend the region either. New Englanders have a certain snobbery about understanding what's going on in Europe, in Asia, in South Africa, the latest idea for progressive politics. New Englanders watch for trends, for news, for whatever may get thrown against the castle wall. But I also realize now, several years later, after New England, after South Carolina too, living once again in the Midwest, it is perhaps the New Englanders who are so thoroughly provincial they can't see it. When I was living in western Massachusetts, the people in Albany (less than two hours away) were not people like us. The people in Boston (an hour and a half to the east) were a different species. The people in Vermont and New Hampshire and Connecticut and Rhode Island, to say nothing of New York and Pennsylvania, weren't even in the same phylum. In a very real way the Berkshires were the borders of our honest sympathies.

When you live in the Midwest, however, a few hours' drive for dinner is nothing. Detroit Lakes is an hour east of Fargo, but people will drive to Detroit Lakes when they're out because that's where they happen to point the car. Longer trips, in good weather, are almost as easy. In bad weather we all carry emergency survival gear to keep us warm when the blizzards bury the car. Yet no one says very much if you drive four hours from Fargo to Minneapolis to see a show, attend a reading, then drive right back. It happens all the time.

The four-hour drive to Winnipeg is a similarly easy journey. When the landscape opens up, your perception opens with it. When you live on the prairie, you understand that Fargo and Winnipeg and Sioux City and Sioux Falls and Jamestown and Minot and Fergus Falls and Detroit Lakes are all parts of the same community. In November and December, the same Arctic wind hits those towns. In summer, the same sun and rain raise our crops and dreams. We have things to share—the same sense of isolation, the same sense of hope, the same sense of needing to touch someone else, to make sure you share your thinking, to make sure you know they're there. And if they don't think like you do, you can talk about it, you can engage those people. Prairie people are not isolated, despite the physical distances between them. There is the act of reaching out.

Perhaps the Pacific Ocean and large bodies of water in general share those things with the prairie. Once you're there, you can't help but look at the great deal around you, the stars you can see, who else is here, what else is going on, what does that going on have to do with me, what can I learn from those other people. Great expanse can make friends faster than the body press of city life. That much is certain.

HAWAII COMES. From my seat, looking beyond the woman sitting next to me, I cannot see the shore approach. Nor the city lights. Nor the harbor. My first glimpse is runway lights, then the terminal.

One hour. That's how long I have. The middle of night for me, I have no idea what the local time is. We all get off the plane, move from one departure gate to another, sit in chairs less comfortable than those in Fargo.

I walk outside and breathe a deep, tropical breath. Palm trees grow on the other side of a short concrete wall that guards the far edge of the drive. The moon is new tonight, so I cannot tell what I'm looking at. It could be the side of a hill or the horizon of the ocean. There is no birdsong. No traffic either. Even the concession shops and stands are closed. The other passengers and I look at each other; one man asks me how I like Hawaii so far. I tell him it's terrific. We laugh at the polite irony. I've promised Maureen I would send a postcard from here, but even that's impossible. The speakers in the ceiling soon let me know my next flight is boarding.

The tremendous rush of a 747 taking off, then the darkness again. Then drinks. Then dinner. Then another movie. Then sleep. Technologies and miracles have made it possible to ignore Hawaii. Under way again.

Already out of context, I am leaving my own country now. So many departures toward this next arrival. How much of home is too much in a new place? How much will that next place rise up to meet a newcomer's feet? That's the real thrill, you see. There's no way to know.

AT THE HANGI

Rotorua—Day One

TODAY, I AM IN ROTORUA. AND TODAY, I FEAR, I AM THE MOST common, obvious, ignorant type of tourist. I have a camera slung around my neck, and my face has frozen in a type of silly, incongruous grin.

The InterCity bus left Wellington early this morning under the still-dark predawn sky. Sleep came easy in the rocking coach, despite the passing views of the rocky western shores of the North Island of New Zealand and the Tasman Sea beyond them. I wish I had stayed awake.

We stopped for a break in the town of Taupo, and I took the fifteen minutes to walk around a bit and stretch my legs. Had I been awake in the bus, I would have known what to expect when I came around a shop corner and caught sight of Lake Taupo, immense and shimmering in the midmorning light. In the southwestern distance beyond the lake, two old black volcanoes rose to snow-covered peaks. Mount Tongariro and Mount Ruapehu. Mount Ngauruhoe was also there, in the clouds. We drove right by them, the bus driver told me. Quite a sight, he said, even having passed them a thousand times on his routes.

A brochure I found at the Taupo Information Centre says the lake was created by one of the planet's largest geophysical events: "The Taupo eruption, one of the biggest volcanic eruptions that has occurred in the world in the last 5000 years, took place in A.D. 186. Ash erupted up to 1000 km in the atmosphere and was recorded by both the Chinese and Romans."

I kicked myself for having slept through this.

Still, no time to linger, or to explore. There were schedules to keep, so we boarded the bus again and headed for Rotorua. Green hills out every window. Water in rivers and small streams and dripping from leaves. And what I had assumed was a remaining mist from last night's rain I discovered was not. Not even close.

As the bus wound its way into the city, the countryside literally steamed—white clouds rising from small pools and thermal springs in the hillsides. Already I regretted the fact that I've only planned a day and a half in this town. No time for just wandering the streets, drinking coffee in some cafe, listening to the melodies of the New Zealand accent as friends share their stories at nearby tables.

Rotorua is a heavily promoted town. A national promise to tourists. There are helicopter and plane rides to look at the volcanic scenery, hot mineral baths to bathe in. Things to do! Things to see! Another brochure tells me there used to be a national wonder near here: the Pink and White Terraces, destroyed in an 1886 eruption of Mount Tarawera, killing one hundred and fifty people and burying villages.

Rotorua is like Yellowstone National Park, a center of geophysical activity and therefore a destination for tourists. They come for holiday, to enjoy the water and mineral baths and scenery. They come to stare at open earth. Unsteady ground, at best.

I check into the Four Canoes Hotel and am greeted by a wonderful desk clerk named Joy. I explain to her my desire to get going quickly, to see what can be seen, to miss very little, somehow already caught up in the pace of a trophy hunter, and soon find myself disembarking from a tourist bus at something called the Agridome—a large dome with a stage and bench seating, a sheep exhibit and show, and a gift shop for tourists. All the varieties of sheep kept in New Zealand are trotted onstage, the quality of their wool and meat explained to the audience. Sheepdogs appear and run up and down the backs of the tolerant sheep, to the applause of the crowd. A sheep is sheared in front of us, and we are allowed to touch the fresh wool, still oily and fragrant. After the show, we are invited outside to watch a dog put some sheep through their trials in a large pen. The whole show takes an hour and a half. At its close, we are put back on the chartered buses and motored away.

It is possible, in New Zealand, to see flocks of sheep on the road being driven by shepherds and dogs from one set of fields to another (what bus drivers call a New Zealand traffic jam), to see sheep dogs and expansive sheep stations, to taste lamb in restaurants and buy wool in shops. And it is possible to remain completely ignorant about it all. There are more than sixty-five million sheep in New Zealand! If anything here is a part of the national identity, it is sheep. While I generally dislike the obvious tourist attractions like this Agridome, this is also an education for me. At least now I can name one or two sheep breeds.

After the Agridome, the tourist bus takes us to the Rainbow Springs Trout Farm, where we see—trout. Also at the Rainbow Springs we enter a Kiwi house and watch both a male and a female stalking about in an artificial night. After Rainbow Springs we motor to Te Whakarewarewa Thermal Reserve to watch Pohutu Geyser erupt, and then we gaze into some of the more than five hundred thermal springs and boiling mud pits, as if we expect something to rise out of the mud.

Te Whakarewarewa contains the New Zealand Maori Arts and Crafts Institute. We walk past a large Maori canoe, Maori houses, a glass-walled exhibit of Maori portraits and clothing. Inside the institute we admire wood carvings on every wall, then tour the perimeter of a large room wherein young Maori men work on carvings in progress. They glance up at us as we pass. None of us on this tour has the courage to ask questions of these men, none of us quite sure if it's proper.

Later, outside the institute, at the far end of the thermal reserve, past the kiosks for ice cream and souvenirs, I am feeling utterly stupid and guilty. I have seen Maori art every single day of this trip. Faces carved into wood, tongues stuck out in what is called a poukena—a gesture designed to distract an opponent during battle. I have seen carved hands of three fingers, representing birth, life, and death, and sometimes a fourth finger as well, for the after-life. I've seen clubs and staffs and paddles. And, here in Rotorua, I'm learning that I've seen nothing.

Back in the States, I meet, chat with, eat with people of color every day. Native Americans, Hispanics, African Americans. Each of them representing a cultural history and heritage that are woven into the context of my community and my life. The fact that we come from different races is obvious, but what we share is much larger than what makes us different, and our conversations almost always concern themselves with what we share, our common goals and dreams and desires, our progress toward or our frustrations with these things.

In New Zealand, I've seen Maori men and women every day, spoken with many of them. And I've simply assumed we share a great deal, which I'm still convinced we do. But the particular foundations of our identities cannot be ignored, and I've been guilty of this ignorance.

Rotorua is considered the capital of Maori life in New Zealand, at least by the Pakeha, despite there being at least thirty-three major Maori tribal districts. *Pakeha* is the Maori word for the non-Maori, mostly white, population of New Zealand. And Pakeha is a term freely adopted by the non-Maori, even when referring to themselves. For tourists, Rotorua is the place to learn about Maori, and I am a tourist here.

Back near the trout farm, there is a gondola ride up a hill to a restaurant overlooking Rotorua and Lake Rotorua, and the island in the middle of the lake. And from there people can rent what is called a luge, a small sled on wheels, the summer version of the ice-track insanity witnessed during the Olympics, and speed halfway down the hill on a concrete track. Or, people can hang onto an overhead bar and swing down a zip-line, as if they were in para-trooper training. And, of course, there's bungee jumping too.

I eat lunch in the cafeteria-style restaurant overlooking the is-land and the town and the lake, and when I am done a taxi brings me back to the Four Canoes Hotel. When I walk in, a story is circu-lating about a guest—a young girl who decided, with her father, to ride the luge. The luge can get going fairly fast, I'm told. People pilot their sleds with an aggressiveness you would never see on a road, bouncing each other, jostling each other, speeding around embankments. This girl and her father took a corner too fast, tried to pass another rider. They went face-first into the track, their sled heading off into the wild blue. No helmets. No padding of any kind. The girl's face was bruised heavily where it met the concrete, as were her arm and leg.

I asked her if the ride was worth it.

"Oh," she said, "certainly."

I remember an article in an in-flight magazine about how some tourists have come to think of Rotorua as really Rotten-rua because of the omnipresent smell of sulfur. The author was debunking that idea, proclaiming Rotorua a fine town, a clean town, an admirable town. It's true that the odor of sulfur is everywhere in Rotorua, the thousand or more vents and mud pits and geysers and thermal springs leaving no small grove or corner unfilled. But Rotorua is a complicated place.

There is no shyness here about tourism. In the Yellow Pages of the phone book there are six and one-half pages of hotels in Ro-torua—from the Aaron Court Motel to the Wylie Court Motor Lodge. In every hotel and shop there are flyers and advertisements for the Skyline Gondola, hovercraft rides, paddleboat rentals, fishing trips, Maori shows in the hotels or at a marae. A hundred ways to spend the tourist dollar. Yet, there is also the feeling that something real and large and important pushes against the tourist facade. Just as there is a great deal more to Yellowstone National Park than the group of tourists snapping pictures of Old Faithful, or just as there is a great deal more to the history of the American West than can be found at the Buffalo Bill Museum, there is more to Rotorua. Perhaps because of the inescapable tourist sights and events here, the hint of real depth is strong and persistent. Even at McDonald's—which I wander into to get a fast cup of coffee as I stroll to the lake to get a look at the black swans paddling the townsite shore—wooden Maori carvings make up the posts and pillars, the entirety of one wall.

Rotorua—Day Two

OK. How do I say this?

Just before supper time last night, a small group of us assembled in the foyer of the Four Canoes Hotel. Each of us had reservations for a Maori hangi. None of us had been to one before. We made small talk, paced about the lobby wondering what this evening would bring.

I'd picked up a thin black book in the afternoon, *Kawe Korero: A Guide to Reporting Maori Activities,* by Michael King, and so this much I knew in advance.

Reporting Maori occasions

Most Maori public functions that journalists will have to attend or report will take place on a marae. They will include hui, conferences, tangihanga, karakia, perhaps even weddings and twenty-first birthday parties. In all these instances, visitors are put through a welcoming or "decontamination" ceremony. This varies slightly in detail from district to district and from marae to marae. But the basic structure is the same and journalists should be familiar with it and understand it, so as to feel confident and to know how to respond if they are part of it. In some (but by no means all) instances, it begins with the wero or challenge, carried out by a man wielding a taiaha.

The explanation that follows is given by an authority on Maori ceremonial, Ranginui Walker.

"The wero . . . is a cultural survival from the times of tribal conflict. Its purpose was to determine whether visitors came with friendly or hostile intent. Accordingly, as the challenging warrior went through his gestures of defiance he never took his eyes off the visitors—if they were hostile one of the fastest runners among them could break ranks to pursue and kill him before he made the safety of the pa. Today the wero is performed in honour of VIPs. The leader who picks up the dart placed before the visitors signifies peace, whereupon the party is led on to the marae.

"A party of visitors arriving at a marae may not enter unannounced because they are waewae (sacred feet). They bring with them alien tapu and accompanying ancestral spirits which might be inimical to those of the tangata whenua (hosts), so they must assemble at the entrance to await the karanga (call). This is announced by the high-pitched wail of women paying tribute to the dead. As visitors walk on, their eyes are cast down in homage to the dead.

"Once on the marae, the visitors halt with a clear space separating them from the hosts, where both stand for a few minutes in acknowledgement of their mutual bereavements as well as those of other tribes. At a signal from the hosts visitors are free to sit down. The elders sitting on the paepae (formerly the beam on the threshold of the meeting house but nowadays a bench off to one side) rise in turn to give speeches of welcome.

"The mihi (welcome) has a standard format. It begins with

a tauparapara (chant in poetic form which identifies the local tribe). Depending on the occasion the tau may be a tribute to the dead or a philosophic exhortation to the living to unite in harmony.

"The second part of the mihi is the eulogy to the dead. Reference is often made to recent bereavements of the hosts, visitors and other tribes. This part of the mihi is embellished by mythological allusions and figures of speech which indicate the oratorical prowess of the speakers. They are poetic, deeply spiritual and very touching.

"The third part of the mihi is introduced by a clear separation between the living and the dead. The dead are farewelled and consigned to the spirit world. The orator then turns to greet the living. Greetings are extended to the canoes, the tribes, the four winds. Individual visitors of note are welcomed by name. At this point it is usual to make reference to the reason why the two groups have come together (kaupapa).

"The mihi concludes with a waiata (song), often a lament but sometimes one that identifies the speaker's tribe and the notable landmarks in his territory. The whaikorero (speech in reply) by a visitor also follows the format of the mihi. At the conclusion of the speeches intimacy between the hosts and visitors is expressed by physical contact through shaking hands and pressing noses (the hongi). The food provided for visitors immediately after the formalities signifies the complete ritual decontamination of waewae tapu. The visitors are then free to mingle with their hosts."

Then Newt came through the door. Newt, of course, is Maori. He's a good-looking man, just under six feet tall, with a disarming grin and a loud, energetic voice. His is the type of energy that transfers itself to others. The nervousness of the hotel company soon changed into a type of summer-camp giddiness.

"You all are going to the hangi tonight?" he asked.

There were a few nods and yeses.

"Choice!" he cried. "Let's go!"

Newt led us to a small bus, drove to one or two more hotels to pick up others, and then we were leaving Rotorua, driving into the steaming hillsides.

"So," he boomed into the bus's microphone, "how many of you are from the United States?"

A few of us raised our hands.

"Choice!" cried Newt.

Every time he said "Choice" there was a bit more laughter on the bus.

"Anyone here from Australia?"

A couple in the back of the bus said they were.

"Choice!" cried Newt.

He went through a list of likely countries—England, Japan, Korea—making us laugh, and pointing out, I thought, that none of us were from here.

"What do you all think of Te Aotearoa so far?" he asked.

People clapped, said they loved it, smiled broadly.

"We don't call this place New Zealand, you know," he said, drawing out the *Zealand* so it sounded like a buzz saw. "That's Dutch. You're in Maori land now, so it's Te Aotearoa, the Land of the Long White Cloud."

A few of us tried to get out mouths to say "Te Aotearoa."

"OK now," he said, "there are some things we need to talk about, to go over, so that none of you fine tourists gets killed tonight and winds up as part of the dinner."

His own laugher was the loudest at this one.

"In the days of our tupunas, our ancestors, you see, when one tribe of Maori would go to visit another tribe, they would arrive in a large canoe, what we would call a waka. You need to imagine that we are a tribe of our own, and this bus is our waka."

The people on the bus all quietly said, "Waka."

"Now when a visiting tribe would show up in their wakas, the people they were visiting didn't know if they were coming as friends, or if they were coming to start a war. So there is a type of ceremony at the start of a visit to determine what is what. Have you all selected a rangatira, a chief, yet?"

"No," we said.

"Well, you need to do that. You need to select who is going to lead this waka."

Instantly we selected a man named Kelly, the tallest and most strongly built man in the bus.

"Kelly, you going to be the rangatira, the chief?" Newt asked.

"I guess so," Kelly said.

"Choice!" Again, more laugher.

"Now, Kelly," Newt continued, "when we get there, everyone else must walk behind you. Got that, everyone? No one walks in front of Kelly. You don't want to start a war tonight. Kelly, my man, when we get there, you're going to have to face what we Maori call a wero, a challenge. One of the men at this marae will come out swinging a very large club, called a taiaha. What he wants to do is scare you, OK? He wants to show that if this waka wants a war, they're up to it. When he gets right up to you, he'll place a gift at your feet. When he does this, you have two options. You can pick it up, which means this waka is coming in peace, or you can step on it, which means you're here for a war. If you step on it, everyone else duck, because the next thing you'll see is Kelly's head rolling on the ground. And don't look for me, because I'll be driving this waka back to town at top speed. Kelly, please pick it up, OK?"

"OK!" said Kelly.

"Choice!" said Newt.

The bus rolled into the deepening twilight, off the main road onto ever smaller and more narrow side roads.

"Now here's what's going to happen after the wero," Newt said. "There will be singing, and you all will be welcomed onto the marae. When you go into the meetinghouse, only men can sit in the front rows, OK? Sorry, ladies, but that's the way it is. Only men in the front row. If this were a traditional marae, you all probably know that you couldn't wear your shoes inside or take pictures, but don't worry about that. After some more singing, you'll be welcomed with a mihi, some formal speech making. Kelly, as rangatira you'll have to stand and say something for your waka about how nice it is to be here. Any of the other men here, if you feel you want to, you can rise and say something as well. But only men can make a speech, OK? Ladies, there's a part of this evening that's for you as well, so don't worry, but I'm not going to tell you what it is yet. I think I'll let that be a surprise. Then after the speech making, all you need to do is sit back and enjoy the show. OK? Choice! Then it's time to eat!"

Newt's voice and enthusiasm had every one of us in the bus believing we really were in some type of modern waka. Briefly I wondered what the women on the waka thought about the roles they were, or were not, going to play tonight, but I marveled at the transformation taking place inside our waka-bus. Each of us knew, somewhere in our heads, that we were simply part of a never-ending series of tourists bused out to the countryside for a night of Maori culture. Yet, each of us also knew that we were about to take part in an old custom, a custom with a cultural importance that Pakeha could only hope to partially understand. Easy tourism or primer for the ignorant, quietly I was thrilled.

Newt got us all singing old camp songs as the waka continued its journey. We sang drinking songs, children's songs. Then Newt told us we would have to offer a song, as a group, back to our hosts at one part of the evening. "How about 'O Susanna'?" he asked. "You all remember that one?"

"'O Susanna'?" I thought. Surely the Pakeha musical world has enough in common for something else? Someone on the bus suggested "Amazing Grace" instead, and Newt said that would be choice as well. We gave it a trial run-through, giggling at the variety of keys we started in.

The bus drove around a final corner and brought us to the shore of a lake, dark yet reflecting the newly risen moon.

"Choice!" Newt exclaimed once more. "We're here!"

A few paces back from the beach, the beginning of the marae. There was a sidewalk separating a neat lawn and leading some forty yards back to the meetinghouse itself, which was built in the traditional A-frame style, large wooden and heavily carved beams placed in the ground at each side and soaring to cross in the middle. We stepped off the bus and quickly made sure Kelly was in the lead. Newt said we were waiting for two other wakas, so for a few minutes we milled around. Newt told us to make sure we didn't actually step on the marae, and we were only too glad to follow his instructions. Finally, the other wakas arrived. Newt told the other drivers that we were going to sing "Amazing Grace" instead of "O Susanna," those drivers told their passengers, and we were ready for the night to begin.

All told, there were fifty of us carefully standing behind Kelly, who stood, obviously nervous, at the end of the sidewalk, at the threshold of the marae. A company of ten Maori men and women, dressed in traditional reed outfits—skirts for the men, a straight strapless dress for the women—emerged from the meetinghouse. Suddenly, there was a loud shout from the Maori, and one man began to make his way toward us. In his hands, a long taiaha shaped like a very thin canoe paddle, which he swung broadly, high and low, with great speed and force. This taiaha, I saw, could remove a head from shoulders easily.

The warrior's approach to us was a dance, a ritualistic series of high steps, hops, turns to each side. The taiaha whirled around him. His eyes bulged and his tongue stuck out—gestures to distract an opponent. Effective, certainly.

For five minutes the warrior approached us, and though I'm sure he was nearly blinded by the camera flashes pointed at him in the darkness of the evening, he was an intimidating presence. Kelly, to his credit, stood motionlessly. Newt stood by his side, ready to instruct.

When the warrior came within six feet of Kelly, he threw a fern leaf at Kelly's feet, then slowly backed away. When Newt said it was OK, Kelly bent down and picked up the fern. Not a few of us, I'm sure, were imagining the possibility of his stepping on it, and there was an audible sigh when he held it safely in his hand.

The warrior looked at him, then made a slow sweep of the taiaha low in front of this evening's rangatira. The warrior slapped his thigh, and from the step of the meetinghouse the other men and women began singing. A wonderful song, lilting and melodious, in the Maori language.

Once inside the meetinghouse, arranged like a small auditorium with rows of chairs facing a slightly raised stage at the far end, men filled the front row. We heard a mihi, a welcoming speech, in Maori, translated into English by one of the men on the stage. When it came time for us to offer return speeches of welcome, Kelly rose and said how nice it was to be here, how much he was looking forward to the evening. His speech was met with a loud Kia ora, which means both hello and acknowledgment. A gray-haired and bearded man dressed in khaki rose, explained that he was from South Africa and would like to give a greeting in the language of his place, Afrikaans, which he then translated himself. He made a point of the fact that New Zealand, Te Aotearoa, and South Africa share the same stars in the sky, perhaps a great deal more as well. His welcome was met with another loud and, it seemed to me, honest Kia ora. I rose and made a short speech, taking the South African's cue, about coming from a place where the stars are very different, yet coming to learn and share, about desiring to bring back with me something real to share in my own community. I'm sure I was guilty of sentimentality, at best. Still, the Kia ora made me feel like I'd said something good.

After the speeches, the Maori men and women sang war songs and love songs. The men demonstrated how to use various long and short weapons. There was an intricate choreography of stick throws amongst three kneeling women while the rest sang a happy song. The women untied poi, balls of flax on long and short strings, from their belts, and offered several songs that included swinging poi, the balls striking open palms in perfect unison and in time with the music. Then the Pakeha women were invited onto the stage to give a try at swinging the poi themselves. Pakeha women, we quickly learned, need practice.

After the men were invited onto the stage to try a war dance or two, to stick our own tongues out in a poukena and demonstrate our own need for practice, and the whole room's laughter grew softer, each of us was invited onto the stage for a type of receiving line, a hongi. In a hongi, you shake the hand of whom you are meeting, and press noses as well. A moment of intimacy, nicely done.

The singing continued for an hour, we did our best with "Amazing Grace," and then we were invited outside to look at the uncovering of the hangi. The hangi is a feast cooked underground. Large rocks are heated in an intense wood fire, then placed in a pit. On top of them meats and vegetables are packed in wire cages, then covered by leaves or blankets and finally dirt. The juices in the foods mingle with each other and the rocks to create a steaming cooker. There is no seasoning. We had beef and pork and lamb and squash and pumpkin and then more vegetables and seafood. It was, of course, tremendously good. And when the feast was over, there was a song of farewell. The Maori women running the dining room sang "Amazing Grace," too. Then our coach was waiting for us.

On the way back into town, Newt had us singing every song he could think of. And we sang loudly, badly, forgetting a lot of the words, happily, enthusiastically.

Leaving the bus, thanking Newt for all his energy, I wandered back into the Four Canoes Hotel too filled with the night to head straight off to bed. I decided to have a drink in the hotel bar.

There were two men already at the bar when I found my own stool. One was Polynesian, from Fiji, the other was Maori. They were married to two Pakeha sisters, and while the women talked about those things that sisters talk about, the men had retired to the bar to watch a bit of rugby on the television and to entertain each other with their memories.

"You were at a hangi?" asked the Fijian. "Did the food come in tin foil from the hotel kitchen?"

Tourism, I thought to myself, can create lies as well as access.

"No," I said, then told them the story of the evening.

SO FAR FROM HOME

1. Queenstown

IS IT POSSIBLE TO COME HOME TO A PLACE YOU'VE NEVER BEEN?
How many new ways is it possible to fall in love?

I am sitting this morning on a large rock in the shadow of a row
of poplar trees, on the shore of a lake named Wakatipu, just outside
a small town called Queenstown, in a region called Otago, on the
South Island of a country named New Zealand. It's a cold morning
and I'm fairly bundled up. I've brought some coffee from the youth
hostel, where I'm staying, and its steam rises to my face. The dawn
is almost complete. The clear blue crystal water breaks in small
waves over the gravel beach.

I'm about as far away from the place at least the mailman thinks
he'll find me as I can be, yet—let's say it honestly—I'm suddenly
feeling more at home here, at the shore of this lake, at the feet of
these mountains, than I've felt in a very long time. And I don't
know why.

Wakatipu is a mountain lake, not so very far across but very
long and winding, the only flat surface in otherwise rugged country. In the short distance to the east from my rock perch, a range of

mountains called the Remarkables drops their sheer faces into the lake. Angular and jagged, unforested, cut and broken with a thousand small valleys and rifts, these peaks this morning are snow covered and cloud capped, dirt brown and slate blue and snow white all. In places, the sun comes in and illuminates a wall or valley, turning a field of snow and ice into a beacon, a rock face into a mural of colors, the morning into theater.

When you think of the Definition, the Thing itself, the picture in the dictionary, you think of mountains like the Remarkables. It's got everything to do with size and weight, with comparing a less than six-foot-tall human body with the leaps of a mountain face, with placing human time next to earth time, with feeling quite small, with feeling like you're going to fall into the abyss and love every minute of it.

To my right, much closer but across the lake, the more rounded Mount Cecil and then Walter's Peak catch what sunlight can break through the cloudy sky. Snow comes about halfway down Mount Cecil. Grasslands go about halfway up. Sheep graze Walter's Peak.

How can I talk about Queenstown? If you're standing at the waterfront, looking right, left, straight ahead, or around to the back, you look into mountains. You look at hard rock and begin to get a sense that this place wasn't easy to get to. But once you do manage to get here, once the passage has been found, once the trails have been made, you also see this is a place you must get to. There's something—I don't want to say spiritual—*personal* about Queenstown.

Perhaps my reaction is just one of contexts, the prairie kid suddenly in the hills. But I don't think so. I've been in lots of mountains before. Something about Queenstown is different.

When I break myself away from the shore and walk the waterfront, I pass the ticket and information center for the TSS *Earnslaw*, an old coal-fired steamer, built in 1910, that takes people over for a day at Walter's Peak, for a day at a sheep station and a meal on the water. I pass signs for air trips around Milford Sound, a fjord on the South Island's west coast. I pass docks where half a dozen companies promote their jet-boat rides.

In town itself, shops promote horseback riding, mountain-bike rentals, and bungee jumping. There's Eichardt's Tavern, the Queenstown Bay Centre, art galleries, the ANZ Bank, the Park Royal Hotel, Te Aotearoa New Zealand Souvenir Shop, antiques, wool shops, Queenstown Bay Trading Company, the Hide Shop. Above and behind them all, of course, there are the mountains.

Helicopters buzz overhead, taking tourists on sight-seeing excursions, or off to jet boats on a particularly wild part of the Shotover River. Jet boats buzz in and out of the harbor, making a grand, explosive, tight circle as they come in. Fishing excursions get ready to go. Water taxis roam about. There are autumn colors in the trees that line the inlet and edge up the mountainside, the dark green of the conifers in often brilliant contrast. There's snow on every peak.

Queenstown *is* a tourist town, but not the American version. There is a McDonald's, there's a Kentucky Fried Chicken and a Pizza Hut, but they're discreet, not loud. There are no billboards in the hills, and there aren't any go-cart tracks; there aren't a hundred thousand cheap little ways to spend your money that have nothing to do with where you are. New Zealanders are not the type of people who want to ride a go-cart around a small oval track that could be as easily in Peoria as Kathmandu. What they do, they do honestly—and I don't mean in terms of cheating. When you get on the water, damn it, you're going to get on the water. When you go up in the mountains, you *go up* in the mountains.

Most New Zealanders, I believe, are pacifists, but there's very little about their energy that's pacific.

I spend my day getting bearings, looking in windows, finding my way about. I ride the skyline gondola up one of the mountains behind the city, 450 meters to the top, and I have lunch in the coffee shop there, looking out over Queenstown and Lake Wakatipu toward the Remarkables. What can I say about this? I'm as impressed as I can be with just the geography.

I call home to my wife, Maureen.

"So *tell* me about it," she says.

I do my best to describe what the town looks like, how the mountains shape the shoreline, and what I feel about it all, but I do a lousy job.

"It's heaven," I say toward the end of my description. "I can't tell you how happy I am to be here."

"You miss me that much, huh?"

Another silly mistake.

"What's going on there?" I ask.

"Nothing. *Nothing* is happening here."

I suspect she's wrong. I suspect there's a great deal going on at home. But I suspect there's little new. She's living in our routine while I am happily outside it. Every step I take puts my foot in a place it's never been before, brings me to things I've never seen, adds something fresh to my own history. Her steps are replays.

I tell her I love her, that I miss her terribly, that what I really want is for her to be here with me, for Kate and Andrew to be here with both of us, but it's almost lame. When we hang up, I exit the phone booth and walk around a corner so I can see the lake again and Mount Cecil rising from the far shore. It's twilight, and the water has turned purple. Mount Cecil is a dusky brown. The Remarkables, however, catch the setting sun long after it's set in town, and they explode that light. I take the deepest breath I can, let it out as slowly as possible.

⤙

IT's EVENING NOW, almost dark. There is a black-and-white cocker spaniel running around, a golden retriever sitting on the back of a jet boat. Kiwi children run about the harbor shore, playing.

The entrance to the Queenstown Harbor is split by a long sandbar. There's a post at the end of it with an aqua-green light on top marking the limit of safe travel. The jet boats have come in, making their turns close enough to the light post that passengers could touch it. The *Earnslaw* has come in. Ducks have congregated at the shoreline. Some are feeding, some are bathing themselves. The carts that sell coffee, cappuccino, stuffed baked potatoes are closing up. The crowds are clearing. The sun has set behind the mountains. But through the clouds, a patch of sun moves slowly up Mount Cecil, then the Remarkables. Wood smoke rises from people's chimneys and from autumn-leaf fires burning. In the distance I can hear the sound of a single chain saw.

People walking the waterfront are most often couples. Two women, a man and a woman, a woman with several children. Two German shepherds play at chasing ducks in the shallows.

There is a wishing well at the waterfront, a stone well with a little roof over the opening. The sign on it says, "Wish for your return to Queenstown."

The lights are coming on—the cabin lights, the pub lights, the balcony lights at the Park Royal Hotel. On the pedestrian shopping street there's a little less traffic. It's time to move in for the meal.

At night in Queenstown, amber and white house lights, street-lights, dot the hillside looking out over the lake. Only the green sandbar light casts a reflection. Waves come up on the shore, the wind rustles in the trees, traffic moves occasionally on the streets. The Southern Cross is almost directly overhead.

Behind Mount Cecil the Southern Lights begin a display. They begin gently as just a faint glow, as if the moon were trying to rise from the west, causing the mountains to become a silhouette. As the evening grows deeper they get brighter, more dynamic. A small group of men and women walking the waterside stop near me to watch. They *ooh* and *aah* when the curtains and sheets of color are most intense. One of them starts to applaud, then they all join in. Even me, quietly.

A WARM DAY after a cold night. The Remarkables are brilliant! The surrounding hills seem electric in autumn colors. Branches from a giant willow tree near the waterfront swing in the breeze, brush themselves into the poplars. Tandem parapenters—a type of sky-diving where you strap yourself to an "instructor," then jump off a cliff with a parachute already open for a ten-minute glide over and through the landscape toward a landing on a rugby field—float off the mountain behind the gondolas rising from the city to the Sky-line restaurant and observation deck.

I want to see the parapenters land, so I take a taxi from the town center back to the hostel to get my camera and then race to the rugby field in time to see them finish their descent. The taxi driver hears my voice, asks me where I'm from, asks me what I think about Queenstown so far. I tell him I like this area, this country, very much. He says that's good to hear. He thinks people around here are different from the rest of the New Zealanders. People around here aren't so caught up in every little thing that bothers other Kiwis, he says. I tell him I understand why, that it makes sense to me.

Just off the rugby field where I'm standing there's a horse in someone's yard, grazing. Above me the yellow parachutes spin in lazy circles over the green pine-forest hills. There are three of them now. When they finally approach the field I see the clients are three college-age women. As they near the ground their faces are tight lipped, wide eyed, filled with determination, remembering, I'm sure, whatever instructions they were given about how to land and not tangle their legs with the man behind them. Once they land, however, it's all smiles and hugs and cries of "We did it! Wow! What a sight! Did you . . . ?"

Their reactions are important to me. While I have no desire to leap off a cliff strapped to someone else and a parachute, I have bought a ticket that will take me out of town, through some mountains to a fairly remote part of the Shotover River, out to Skipper's Canyon where people hurl themselves off a bridge with a glorified rubber band attached to their legs, where the world's highest bungee jumping that's not from a helicopter or balloon takes place.

Bungee jumping started in New Zealand. I don't know if I'm going to jump yet. But I know I want to see it.

⤿

It's sometime just after noon, and after an aimless walk around town I'm standing in the shop where you sign up for bungee jumping. A. J. Hackett Bungy, it's called, after the man who supposedly started it all. If I wanted to, I could sign up for whitewater rafting, jet boating, helicopter trips through canyons, parapenting and tandem skydiving, all sorts of dangerous thrills. Videos play from monitors in the two main rooms showing happy people doing crazy things to themselves.

Everyone in here has either just come back from some adventure or is waiting to go. The differences between the two groups are clear and immediate. The survivors are relaxed, talk loudly, watch the videos of their own leaps of faith made just an hour before, point out the smallest details to those who were with them. Those who are waiting to go are wound tighter than clocks. Their smiles are quick and nervous. They too watch the monitors, more closely than those who've gone before, but the details are lost in the act of imagining their bodies in the place of the one flailing about in midair on the screen.

A beige Land Rover pulls up to the curb, and a man gets out to collect us. There are nine of us, it seems. Three women and six men. We all get in, and the truck pulls away from the shop, away from Queenstown, off onto a dirt road leading through the mountains.

Quickly, I discover I can't spend time creating an imaginary fear of leaping off a bridge—I am more worried about this road! One-lane wide, almost, this road is cut into the hillsides, sometimes muddy, sometimes covered with a thin sheet of frost or ice. There are no guardrails to keep us from the drop-offs, which often fall away from the road down several hundred feet. The brown and green and then snowcapped hills we're driving through are dramatic and sharp, but I'm not spending very much time looking at them. Our driver—he told us his name, but I can't remember it—is very casual with his driving. I can't get used to his being on the right side of the car. Every corner is a blind corner.

I'm sitting sideways on a bench in the back of the Land Rover, and all I can think about is what would happen if we were to slide off the road, the tumbling and flipping, the multiple fractures and certain death.

We stop three times on our way to the bridge. Two of the stops are to enjoy the scenery, rock formations with improbable names like the Upside Down Elephant, and mountain valleys cut deeply into tussock. At the first of these, a few of the men run behind a large rock to relieve themselves. The other stop is to deliver mail at a remote sheep station. As we drive, the driver asks us if we have questions, but the only question that gets asked is about height. Is this cliff or this drop-off as high as the bridge? we ask. No, he says, the bridge is much higher. Each of us in the Land Rover laughs, but it's not from good humor.

Finally, the bridge. Skipper's Canyon is deep and narrow, sheer rock faces cut into the hills. At the bottom, the Shotover River looks only inches deep. The rocks are clearly visible, which is not comforting. The bridge itself is one lane, a brown steel suspension bridge. It's roadbed is wooden. As we drive across it, initial exclamations of "Wow!" or "Shit!" give way to silence inside the Land Rover. It's 229 feet from the bridge to the water.

We turn around just beyond the bridge and walk back to its center where four or five instructors are waiting for us. There's a scale for weighing us (we were also weighed at the shop in town, and our weight is marked with blue felt pen on the backs of our hands), and there are several very long bungee cords. More immediately, however, there is this distance from the bridge to the bottom.

Intellectually, I know things look higher from the top than they do from the bottom. Standing at the top of a swimming pool high dive gives a much different perception than standing under it. But knowing this does not help the feeling of endless space below this bridge. Knowing this does not make the fear go away.

An American woman named Tana is the first to go. She and some of her friends played rock-paper-scissors to see who went first. She gets a towel around her ankles, some nylon wrapped around the towel, the bungee cord attached with a metal hook to the nylon. Feet bound, she shuffles to the end of a small platform built onto the bridge. One of the instructors lets go of the cord, which gives a small tug at her feet and the both of us a nearly coronary seizure.

"You want to jump out as far as you can," an instructor says. "You want to get a type of pendulum effect. If you jump straight down you'll go like a yo-yo, just down and then boing right back up."

"You want me to jump out?" Tana asks.

"As far as you can."

The instructors start a countdown, and we all join in. Five, four, three, two, one, Bungee!

Off she goes. No hesitation at all. A five-foot-tall woman with short dark hair has just leaped from a bridge, and everyone around me is smiling. There's no sound from the canyon, either. No screams, no terror. Just this woman falling and falling and falling.

When she gets near the bottom, when the cord begins to stretch and pull her away from a bloody death on the riverbed rocks, she starts to yell. I can't tell if she's speaking words or pronouncing something more urgent and physical, but I can tell her cries are happy ones. She must have jumped out away from the bridge as the instructor told her because when the cord extends its full length she swings under the bridge on her first rebound. Then she appears under us again, falling again, screaming again, having the time of her life. A jet boat appears and answers a question I hadn't thought to ask: how to get down? When Tana stops bouncing, the bungee cord is slowly lowered until the men in the boat can collect her. When she's disconnected, she waves bravely to those of us still above her. The jet boat deposits her on a beach fifty yards downriver.

"Who's next?" one instructor asks.

And it all starts over. The fear, the certainty of death. The same fear that makes me back away from the platform makes a man named Steve step up. He gets the same routine of towel and nylon and cord, the same instructions to jump away from the bridge. In the Land Rover Steve told us he'd jumped before, several times in fact. But it takes three countdowns before he leaves the platform and falls away from us, getting smaller with each second. Then the others go, one by one, no jump any easier for having watched the others. Finally, there's only me and the instructors on the bridge.

"Have you decided if you want to jump?" one of them asks me.

Suddenly the bridge is a very crowded place. Every student I've ever had, those who've hated me as well as those who've liked me, my two brothers and sister and various colleagues and friends are screaming, "Jump! Jump!" My parents and Maureen are screaming just as loudly, "Don't! Don't!" Kate and Andrew are holding their breath. It's a moment for courage and will and inner strength.

"No," I say. "I don't think I will."

I don't get any argument from the instructors, but there's this chorus inside me now whispering, "coward, wimp." When we drive down to the river to pick up the others, they all look at me and say they can't believe I didn't go.

The ride back to town isn't nearly as scary as the ride out; the sheer drops don't look so far down. Everyone talks about what they felt, what they saw, what it was like to fly.

2. Dunedin

NOON. Walking about downtown Dunedin this morning has been the same experience as walking in Manhattan, or Chicago, or any metropolitan area. The buildings are smaller and the air is exponentially cleaner, but the mass of people filling and crowding the sidewalks, then storefronts, the pace of their business, is just the same.

The center of Dunedin is the Octagon, a variation of the town square or circle. The center of it is a small grassy and many-treed park with striped canopy shelters built for catching a bus or taxi. The street that circles the Octagon is itself rimmed by shops and markets. There's the Mackenzie Country Clothing Company, the Civic Centre, Canterbury of New Zealand, the Visitors' Centre, St. Paul's Cathedral, the Warehouse for New Zealand, the Baker's Oven, the Senior Citizen's Club, several others.

The Octagon is built on a hill with St. Paul's toward the top. It slopes downhill from the cathedral toward the Baker's Oven and Ski Barn. Just to the side of the church, on the inside of the roadway, a statue of Robert Burns shows the poet seated on what appears to be a rock. A plaque reports his life span: "Robert Burns, 25 January 1759–21 July 1796." He's a good-looking man, gazing out into the distance toward the harbor. Behind him the cathedral and the hills—around him the sites of a bustling city.

According to *A History of New Zealand,* one of the founders of Dunedin was Reverend Thomas Burns, "a censorious old bigot who was a nephew of the poet. Supported by the Association of the Lay Members of the Free Church, these two [Captain William Cargill was the other] decided to plant a Free Church settlement where 'piety, rectitude and industry' would feel at home, and where the inhabitants as a body would form 'a vigilant moral police.'"

Looking at Robert Burns, sitting in the wake of his nephew, I find myself wondering how a man who dreamed of a moral police would meet the man who penned, "Lord, hear my earnest cry an' pray'r / Against that presbytery o' Ayr." Despite the rain and lowering clouds, Dunedin is made brighter, I think, having placed Robert and not Thomas in its heart.

Things are hopping this noon. The McDonald's (I just poked my head in) is filled with birthday parties for children. This is a town with a hundred coffee shops, most of them single storefronts that tunnel deep back into the buildings, some of them a little more artsy than others, all of them busy. People have lunch outside as well and throw bread to pigeons. The traffic is constant and loud. People park where they're not supposed to. Despite the overcast sky and the occasional rain, it's warmer today than it has been.

Dunedin is not a big city, but it moves like one. Perhaps it's only that I find myself walking about at noontime and happen to have an urgent hunger. Perhaps it's just my own need to see as much as possible of this city in a single day. But I have this feeling that I'm missing everything important.

⤺

Two o'clock. I come up to the Otago Early Settlers Museum on Cumberland Street. On the outside a Romanesque brick building, the portcullis painted orange and purple and blue, on one side there's a train in a room with glass walls. On the inside, the Otago Early Settlers Museum is filled with the things one would expect— the Victorian clothing, the tea services, the diaries, the glassware, the furniture, the uniforms, a few swords and cannons. The train in the glass room is the Josephine. According to the museum litera- ture, the Josephine is New Zealand's oldest preserved steam loco- motive, one of only four Double Fairlie patent models in the world. The others are in Ffestiniog, in Wales.

Other rooms hold the Albion Press, a lighter than previously known letter press, some old penny-farthing bicycles, stagecoaches and train things, a horse whip, an exhibit of contemporary photog- raphy.

There are exhibits of pioneer life: the homes, the utensils, the furnishings, the farm equipment, the flour mills, the shovels. Then there are the whaling try-pots, whaling boats, an exhibit of the shore-whaling stations, a small monument to the laying out of the town by Charles Henry Kettle, the surveyor.

For some reason, I feel farther away from home in this museum than I've felt so far. I know this stuff! This is the history of America, too. This is my own history and folklore. Whaling, frontier life, forestry, even down to establishing a new religious colony and the later gold rush, this history should give me a sense of home. Only the name of the horse has been changed. But it feels like I'm visiting an old family house with new owners. It's all very familiar, and it's all very strange. The heels of my boots echo loudly in each room, and each display reminds me I'm half the planet away from Minnesota.

⤶

THE MORNING BEGINS with breakfast and politics.

The breakfast is several bowls of flakes, muesli, granola, dried and regular fruit, all for the mixing. Milk and cream. Strong black coffee and very hot tea.

The politics begin with sports, mainly the New Zealand national rugby team, the All Blacks (named for their uniforms), and how some years ago they broke the old sports ban regarding South Africa during apartheid. They made a tour of that country, and the South African team made a tour of New Zealand.

"Didn't that bother you?" I ask.

There are several of us at the long head table in the dining room of Knox College, a private dormitory that opens to tourists when the students are away. Andrew Howe, a medical student, is doing most of the talking, explaining what he can.

"It bothered a lot of people," he said. "Riot police were called in when the South African team was here to handle the crowds and demonstrations."

"So why in the world did New Zealand go there, why did they invite that team to come here?"

"Mostly because they have a great team, a real contest."

This isn't a debate, I see, it's a history lesson. Some of us go for toast or more coffee. Somehow the conversation shifts to a more general style of warfare. Andrew explains that New Zealand has historically gone to war with the English, signing on to the time and date of whatever declarations are made. But this creates a bit of an oddity, he says. When England declared war on Argentina over the Falkland Islands, by virtue of geographic placement and time zones, New Zealand did so first. England declared war sometime in the morning. New Zealanders, who were just finishing their suppers, discovered they'd been at war all day.

"And then there's the nuclear problem," he says.

"I thought New Zealand was nuclear free," I say.

"We are. But at least as far as America is concerned, that's the problem."

It seems the States pulled out of a mutual defense treaty among Australia, New Zealand, and the United States when New Zealand declared itself nuclear free and signed the South Pacific Nuclear Free Zone treaty. Or, more exactly, we dropped New Zealand from that alliance. The United States and Australia still cooperate, as do Australia and New Zealand. It's just the Kiwis and the Yanks who don't agree. When New Zealand became nuclear free, the United States sent a warship to make a call at a New Zealand port. New Zealand asked if the ship carried nuclear weapons or ran on nuclear power. The United States has a "neither confirm nor deny" policy when it comes to what may be aboard ships. New Zealand refused entry to the ship, and the treaty was torn.

"Your country decided to push that issue," Andrew says.

My country. People come and go from the table, plans are announced for the day, advice is given and received, fruit and coffee fill plates and cups and then the stomachs of the people who retrieve them. The company is warm and friendly. Outside a steady rain falls, the sound of it occasionally loud through open windows. I feel very far away from my country.

I can imagine the argument for excluding New Zealand. New Zealand happens to sit at a place where not very much happens.

Our national military interest is lower here. In one way, it's a sound military and economic policy.

However. However! My own politics are antinuclear. My own politics are always confused by tangential things like ethics and what I see as our inherent responsibility as a world economic and military power. Sitting at this long table this morning, I remember something said to me at Le Café in Christchurch by a man sitting next to me while we both warmed ourselves with coffee by the fire.

"We don't want to be led by the Japanese. It's not that we don't like them, it's just that their understanding of democracy is young and fairly shallow. We want to be led by the United States."

Democracies depend on dissenting voices. It's a part of the definition. If we're going to be honest about establishing a world democracy, and if we're going to be honest about leading the world in that direction, we're going to have to admit to partnership with those who don't agree. It will cost us money. But it very well could save our souls.

WHAT I FIND MOST REMARKABLE in this museum are the portraits. In the portrait gallery they are everywhere, seven or more rows of them from floor to ceiling. As the sign says on an immaculate eight-station bank table, "The museum has a nationally important collection of original portrait photographs which date from 1860. They include many of Otago's early settler families. The photographs themselves are examples of almost all the known photographic techniques since the invention of photography. Part of the collection is on display in this Edwardian-style presentation, dating from 1908, and many more are in storage. There's an index. Please ask if you want to."

On one wall are Mr. Hugh Frasier Ayson, Mr. and Mrs. Alex Ayson Milton, Alex Johnston, Mr. and Mrs. James Freeman, Mr. and Mrs. John Wilson, Mr. and Mrs. W. Brash, George Hutchison and Mrs. George Hutchison, Thomas and Mrs. Moodie, Mr. and Mrs. Richard Sandilands. The dates here are 1852, 1858, 1848, 1865, 1856.

The people in these pictures do not smile, though in general the women look happier than the men. I know this pose, this expression of determination and will, is a photographic convention, but it makes me wonder about the lives of these men and women. It makes me wonder about what it was like to leave ordered England in the days of Victoria and enter the frontier, to leave a country well established in its contexts and habits and move half the planet away to a country of harder weather, harder homes, harder fields to plow. These are not the smiling pictures of friends. These are pictures of people setting themselves to the task of enlarging the world.

It is impossible to glean a personality from these faces. It is impossible to tell who told jokes, who drank too much, who maintained the moral order. I stare at them for a long time, wishing they would speak louder. I have lots of questions for them today, because I feel so far away myself.

In the same room as the portraits there is something called a polython. A wooden cabinet about six feet tall and three feet wide, the top half of it an arched glass window revealing a large silver disk set on its side. A small boy and his father walk up to it, plunk a coin in a slot, and I discover the polython is really a large music box. Ethereal, wind chime–like music fills the room, and I can almost imagine the faces in the portraits relaxing to a pleasant memory.

༼

FIVE O'CLOCK. I'm in a van that's traveling the shore of Otago Harbor, winding its way the length of the Otago Peninsula toward seals and penguins. The day is still gray and gloomy. The rains are occasional but definite when they come.

I didn't think I'd be able to do this. I'd been told the best time to see the penguins is at sunset, when they come back to shore after a day of feeding at sea, but the regular twilight tour has been canceled for unknown reasons. At the tourist information center, a group of us stood about solemnly, depressed about not getting out to what's called the Penguin Place. Then Nikki, one of the women at the counter, said she knew a tour bus that could take us, if we were willing. Most of us said we were, a phone call was made, and shortly thereafter a van pulled up and we all got in.

Not too far out of Dunedin we discover our van driver is Nikki's mother. This brings a few laughs about calling Mum when you need something done.

"Ah, but she's a good girl," our driver (none of us ever think to ask her name) says. "Did she tell you that she's off to Africa in a wee bit?"

"No."

"She is indeed. She's going to live in tents with some nomads. Next year she wants to go to Antarctica."

The van is quiet now, trying, I'm sure, to imagine Nikki, a young woman who looks like any freshly scrubbed and well-dressed college student in the States, in the wilds of Africa or on the ice of Antarctica. I find myself thinking about Kate, what I would say if she popped into the house one day and said she wanted to spend some time living in a tent or a superinsulated ice station. Would I meet her request with enthusiasm, or would my parental concern make me hesitate, derail her hopes?

Both trips are ones *I* would like to make. However. Nikki's mother says she encourages these trips, thinks they're absolutely marvelous. I admire Nikki's mum.

Nikki's mother is obviously proud of the daughter, yet quite game for an adventure herself. After an hour winding the coast of Otago Harbor at low tide, we pull off the shore road and up to a small white house. This is where we can get a key that will let us pass the fence that surrounds the Penguin Place. The keys aren't so much for security as to gauge how many people are on-site at one time.

Nikki's mum gathers the key and a set of binoculars for each of us in the van while we take the chance to stretch our legs and look at two penguins held in pens here while they recover from some illness or accident. These are yellow-eyed penguins, the rarest in the world. One of them looks fine. The other has an enlarged eye that looks like it could quite simply fall away from its head.

When Nikki's mum has the key and the glasses we're all quickly back in the van and on our way. After five more minutes or so, we turn off the paved road and drive for ten minutes on a single-lane path through the hills. Once again, the simple shape of the landscape captures my breath and imagination. The way one hill sweeps down under brown grass to a hollow or small valley then lifts itself into another hill seems almost magical here. Sheep graze the landscape up to the roadside. One other car passes us, heading back toward town, then all too quickly we find ourselves parked at the top of a bluff. In front of us, the far south Pacific Ocean.

"I didn't think it would be, but this is definitely worth the money!"

This, from Miles, another tourist in the van. We haven't seen a single penguin yet, but he stands near the bluff's edge, looking out to sea. The day's drizzle has lightened, though we can see storm cells moving slowly east.

"You're looking toward Antarctica there," says Mum.

"Wow," says Miles.

We follow a narrow path to our left. Fifty steps from the parking area we come to the top of another bluff that looks down on a broad, protected sand beach. The bluffs form a semicircle around the beach—two hundred yards or more from the bluff we're on to the one on the far side, maybe a hundred yards from the water to the bluff in back. Even with the rain and the strong wind coming off the ocean now, it strikes me as a perfect beach.

"Look at that!"

I'm not sure who says this, but we all find what she's seeing in an instant. A small black shape in the water. It rides a wave to its crest and then jumps, explodes, rockets like the wave gathered it up and shot it, down into the trough between the wave and the one in front of it. These are not small waves. The day is coming just to darkness—and the penguins are coming in.

All I've ever really seen of penguins before are those on television and in zoos, where they waddle awkwardly and look cute. This one penguin, however, is a sleek and very fast animal. It hurls itself from one wave to another, each time taking large leaps between them, looking much more like a fast flying fish than a bird. When it gets to the water's edge, it transforms itself into what we've seen before. It stands, begins the slow waddle, gets knocked down by a larger incoming wave, stands and waddles some more.

Each of us standing on the bluff has our binoculars glued to our eyes. Another penguin appears in the water, and we forget the one on the beach immediately.

We can't get any closer. The penguins are not accustomed to humans. While another access would take us through covered trenches and into blinds, close to the nests in the bluffs surrounding and protecting the cove and beach, a group of people is already there. There are no gift shops, no place to buy film or postcards. Just the wind and water and the site of rare and endangered penguins coming back to land. Two penguins wind their way to the bluffs, and we all stand quietly, too far away for the penguins to hear us even if we hollered, waiting for more.

Over the bluffs from the Penguin Place, at Taiaroa Head, the very end of the Otago Peninsula, is the Royal Albatross Colony, the only mainland albatross colony on the planet. We can't see the rookery from here, but every now and then one of the large birds comes gliding along the shoreline. Binoculars scan the skies, then the waves, then the skies.

After some time we move back to the parking area and then

beyond it to more bluffs on the opposite side. Fur seals rest in kelp beds just below us, on rocks at the waterline, and in the bluffs as well. Their grunting seems to grow louder as the sky grows darker. The simple dirt pathway along the bluff does not separate us. Both below us to our left and above us to our right—every now and then grumbling when someone's flash camera disturbs their slumber—there's nothing between us except the polite advice of Nikki's mum. Focusing my camera on a pup below me, I am launched into an Olympic sprint by a menacing bellow right behind me. A large bull seal I hadn't noticed, hidden in a small overhang, chases me from my spot.

Gray shapes rise and dive in the far distance, and at first we think it might be whales. In this part of the world they would be blue whales or sperm whales. It turns out to be more seals heading toward shore.

Farther down this shore is a colony of spotted shags. The acrobatic birds dart along the bluffs and nest on sheer faces.

Nikki's mum is as engaged by seeing the penguins shoot through waves, by seeing the albatrosses, by coming within inches of fur seals that are not contained or presented for tourist fondling as we are. It's a bleak scene off the coast—gray, hard weather moving in from the southeast, clearly visible miles out to sea—but there is also that sense of the new, of the wonder-full, of the way even the taste of an intaken breath can be a surprise.

We stay until full darkness has made it impossible to see. We return the key and binoculars at McGrouthers Farm, and ride back to Dunedin much quieter than we rode out. Dropped off at Knox College too late for supper, in room 14 I rest on one of the couches and look over the material Nikki handed me at the tourist center.

Yellow-eyed Penguin. *Megadyptes Antipodes.* Height: 32 inches. Weight: 12 lbs. Age: 22 years maximum. Eggs: 1–2. September–November.

Southern Fur Seal. *Arctocephalus Forster.* Weight: 300 lbs. Age: 30 years maximum. Length: 7' maximum. Pups: December–February.

Spotted Shag. *Stictocarbo Punctatus.* Height: 29 inches. Weight: 6–7 lbs approximately. Age: unknown. Eggs: 3–4. September–December.

How far can a person be from home? What are the honest connections we have with a place, with a history or community? This has been an odd day for me. Too much, really, to make sense of. Politics, religion, poetry, commerce, the history of frontier life, the future of seals and penguins and birds. What kind of place can I find for myself? What are my responsibilities to these things? I can imagine spending a lifetime engaged with only a fraction of any single issue.

Or am I looking at it backward? In just this one day it's been possible to come up against all these issues, to meet them and attempt to make some sort of personal sense of them. Where is the border between breadth and depth?

I envy New Zealanders. The size of their country, the closeness of it all, the very-far-away-from-everyone-elseness of it all, lets them see the planet in ways I had not imagined.

Is it possible to come home to a place you've never been?

Of course not. And certainly, yes.

GRAVITY

. . . one of the fundamental forces of nature, the force of attraction existing between all matter. It is much weaker than the nuclear or electromagnetic forces and plays no part in the internal structure of matter. Its importance lies in its long range and in its involving all masses. It plays a vital role in the behavior of the universe.

—*Webster's Encyclopedia*

Six o'clock on a Friday morning in Moorhead, Minnesota, and the thunderstorms quite literally roll over town. Squall lines and gust fronts sneak up over the houses I can see to the west, tumble and bounce over rooftops toward my own home. The top of the bell tower at the Lutheran church on the other side of my backyard disappears into the mist, as if being eaten. Then the mist fades, and I can see daybreak sunshine lighting the tops of roiling thunderheads.

This is a dramatic morning. Standing in the western window of our library at home, what I see could humble a physicist or a theologian. And there are few things I love more than heavy weather, blizzards and windstorms and hard rain all. The simple motion of it over or against the earth.

But, as luck would have it, I'm about to leave. Driving west once again through North Dakota, the Badlands, into Montana, I'll spend the night, perhaps in Billings, perhaps in Red Lodge, then travel south through the Beartooth Pass into Yellowstone, down into Jackson, the Grand Tetons, and, finally, into Park City, Utah, just outside of Salt Lake City. I'm expected to talk to some writers about what happens when their work gets off the page, but I'm not thinking very much about writing this morning. I'm thinking about thunderstorms, rain, and hail. I'm thinking of the way the wind moves over the flatland of the prairie, what damage and beauty that wind can make in storm-time, and I'm thinking of lightning. I'm thinking about how large weather will call me out of bed in the middle of the night, just to watch. I'm thinking about how very pretty the prairie is, how much at home I feel here, and the simultaneous desire I feel each day for a mountain, or an ocean shore. I'm thinking about landscapes and what we want from them.

I hear on the radio news this morning that baseball-size hail fell in western North Dakota, and rainwater runs a foot deep through the city streets of Medora. "Those poor cowboys," the disc jockey says.

Listening to another station, I learn that a plane traveling over southwestern North Dakota on its way to New York was forced to divert to Denver because of turbulence.

In the sky northeast from my window, where I stand with one last cup of coffee before I start an old engine and the land around me moves just a little bit faster than the interstate speed limit, crimson and red—a patch of clear to allow the sunrise through. To the northwest, the gunmetal gray of storm clouds. And to the southwest, some clearing and brightness—a kind of promise for early morning travelers.

I'm taking this trip in no small part because it will take me somewhere I've never been, to the Beartooth Pass, to the northern Wyoming and southern Montana mountains. I've been in mountains before. In the Swiss Alps. In New Zealand's Southern Alps. In the Tombstone Mountains of the Canadian Arctic. In the Blue Ridge Mountains, and the Berkshires, and, yes, in the Rockies before, too. And each visit has filled my head and heart with a very real thrill. Yet, and this much is curious, I've always been very happy to rediscover the flatlands. Each descent from switchback roads and mountain views has lifted my heart. It's good to be home. And then, standing in any one of the many windows of my house, looking at the flatness, my eye has tried to push the visible just a little more than possible. Looking over the wheat fields, I know there are hills in the invisible distance.

So here's a question for you. What do we want from the viewed surface of the earth, from the way the earth rises and falls away, or doesn't? What do our hearts tell us we need from the shape of the land?

If our calendar pictures and postcards are any indication, if the art we frame and hang over our fireplaces and on our bedroom and office walls are any help at all, then it's clear that we are drawn to the dramatic, and from there to the mysterious. Ocean views are dramatic, not only because of their size, but because of their implication. We don't know what's over that horizon, and so our mind is drawn to that wondering. We don't know what's under the surface, the beauty of coral or the simplicity of teeth, and when we find ourselves standing on the beach our mind stares at the potential. Add a whale's spout, however, or sunlight filtering to a school of fish, or the rusting hull of a shipwreck on a sandy floor, or the clear eyes of a leopard seal off the coast of Antarctica—anything, really, to provide a contrasting element—and that contrast, that mystery, captures us. Two textures in seeming opposition.

Likewise, hills and valleys and peaks get matted and framed because their vaulting nature leaves so many edges exposed, so many places to wander or hide. Perhaps I'm wrong about all this, but I suspect that what we find beautiful in nature we find beautiful not only because of its surface, the blue-green of water or the brown-green of rock, but because that surface is a strong hint of some other possibility, some finer detail sure to come.

People who live in the mountains or visit them say, "You can see so far!" Yet, living on the prairie, I know I can see farther. The difference is one, I believe, of a framed and unframed landscape. In the mountains, you see more surface. You see more dirt, more rock; but you see less far. On the prairie you can't see nearly as much surface. The surface falls away with the curvature of the earth, but you can see forever.

If the mountain promises a million specificities, then the prairie promises infinity.

6:30 A.M.

It's funny how you can turn a corner in a town or a village, even one you know very well, and it appears as if the world has changed. As I turn the Jeep westward on the entrance ramp that will take me to I-94 and then through North Dakota and into Montana, the sky becomes the overpowering prospect of the prairie.

There is no sky anywhere on the planet like there is on the prairie. To the north of me, the sky is dark black—clear evidence of rain falling. To the south and to the east, clearing skies and scattered clouds. But as I cross the border into North Dakota what I see to the west is nothing less than wonderful. Remarkable. The clouds look like mountains. Not just *a* mountain, and not just one or two or perhaps even three isolated peaks—but a kind of rolling and massing together. Foothills. Valleys. Ranges. Summits. As I look at the mountains this morning, the cloud mountains over the Dakotas, there are pinks and blues and whites and grays—and it's easy to imagine exploring here. It's easy to imagine a kind of dreamtime hiking. The promise of some new way to arrange the limits of what is possible is, I believe, for each of us, alluring. As I turn a small corner in the highway, though, the top of the sky disappears as I'm thrown into another downpour cell.

Just west of Fargo and Moorhead this morning, the farmland is green. Green pastures of wheat. Green pastures of sugar beets. Green pastures of soybeans. We're too early in the season for the wheat or the barley to adopt their golden hues, too early for the heads of sunflowers to take over the stage. Everything here is young, still leaping upward from the earth. And it's clear this is a healthy place.

I remember a story told to me by two friends, a professor and a student. Standing thigh-deep in a field of young soybeans, the professor was suddenly transfixed by the sky over her farmland while the student, who had parted the tops of the plants and stuck her head below that canopy, was equally amazed. Each of them called to the other, to share their discovery.

Who can say what we want from our landscapes? What kind of gravity calls to our souls? The green flatlands, the rain-soaked streets, the dark sky to the north and still to the west, these mountains of sky and sunlight. For me, at least, each of them is thrilling, dramatic, exciting—choose your own word.

Of course, it makes sense to point out the obvious. No single part of the land we see, the land we find hateful or magical, exists by itself. There is always a context that allows the other to be perceived. If the ground here were not so level, I wouldn't see these cloud mountains. I wouldn't see the tops turning now from a rosy pink to a brilliant white. I wouldn't see, slightly to the south, the dark gray of what looks like fire smoke but I know is only rain.

We are drawn to the mysterious, but the mysterious needs the mundane.

By the time I'm forty-seven miles west of Fargo—a quick stop for coffee in Tower City, then once again an entrance ramp to a westbound highway—the cloud mountains are gone, the torn clouds are gone, the highway steams in full sunshine. In the far distance, though, a kind of grayness and haze; I don't know if I'm seeing the lingering darkness of last night, or storms still in the way. And the ground has changed from the absolute flatness of the Red River Valley. Small rises now, small valleys. My eyes try to catch what's behind each contour or promise.

7:40 A.M.

Just west of Valley City—jet-black sky and lightning to the north—the road narrows to one lane, maximum of fourteen feet wide. There is water from a lake on the interstate highway here, earthen dikes on both the north and the south side of the pavement. The highway is below lake level at the moment. The ground gently rises and gently falls. If I didn't know better, I'd swear the mourning doves try to ride the bow waves of trucks and cars. Red-winged blackbirds scoot across the highway in front of every car. And I find myself wondering if this isn't it, this combination of storm and bird flight and pressing water, isn't what we want—simply proof that the planet still spins.

The morning-show disc jockeys on the radio talk about beer from Belgium.

The cloud mountains have become a thunderstorm. Repeated lightning strikes from sky to earth. As my Jeep and I dip through a small valley, I read a warning sign: "Watch for Water on Roadway." Yet another lake threatens the interstate. On the eastbound side of the highway, a young woman in a sedan has pulled over and cleans her front windshield with a beach towel. I think this is a bit odd, and laugh until I wonder how much water might actually be on the pavement, then suddenly discover the reason she stopped. A cloud of insects—several hundred flattened against the safety glass in seconds. There aren't enough of them to darken the sky, but certainly enough that I can see, in my rearview mirror, the thousands of them swarming. Mayflies.

In Jamestown I pull off for gas and yet another cup of coffee at the McDonald's, and I watch a crane lift a large red billboard to the top of a steel post. The sign urges me to visit White Cloud, the albino buffalo, an animal considered sacred by the plains tribes of Native Americans now become a cuddly, sentimental curiosity to lure road-weary people into town, perhaps long enough to buy more than a cup of coffee and a tankful of gasoline. I ask the lady at McDonald's if she's seen White Cloud yet, and I get a kind of sardonic, half-apologetic/half-embarrassed grin. She says no, she hasn't.

"I wouldn't know what to say," she tells me.

In Jamestown, a fiberglass replica of an American bison—one of the many oversized roadside icons we've come to somehow admire—is locally famous. It shares the same highway as the fiberglass prairie chicken in Rothsay, and springs from the same place as the fifty-five-foot-tall Jolly Green Giant, the armies of wood or steel or fiberglass cowboys and muffler men, and Tommy the thirty-two-foot turtle, who rides a thirty-two-foot snowmobile. Any one of us could pull off at these places, have our pictures taken in the cupped hands of a mammoth Paul Bunyon, then show the pictures to people we might know in Sacramento, or Tallahassee. We could say we'd been on the prairie, and have visual proof. And, frankly, I'm happy people stop to have their pictures taken with the Jamestown bison, which probably won't toss them into the air before sticking a horn through their esophagus.

But the sign urging me to visit White Cloud is something different. White Cloud looks more like a misshapen lamb than a buffalo. And its appeal, at least on the billboard, is cuteness, which is a lie.

107 MILES WEST OF FARGO.

There is a point in every trip when the car and the driver seem to settle into each other and, as a pair, settle into the road. Where the driving itself almost become transparent and you watch the landscape roll by at faster than a mile a minute.

There is a point in every trip when the driving becomes fun.

Bright-silver grain elevators, red barns, cattails in the marshes, red-winged blackbirds, motorcycles, and eighteen-wheel trucks all blend into a kind of moving diorama. From my point of view, I'm sitting still and the world is racing toward and then away from me, and I've got the Rolling Stones on the radio. Clear blue sky in front of me now. I've seen a dozen mountain ranges erupt and then dissipate in the clouds this morning. Lightning strikes, strong wind, mass annihilation of mayflies, and an invitation to see an albino buffalo—and this trip is just beginning.

Already more than one hundred miles west of Fargo, and the landscape here rolls . . . how? To say the landscape rolls "gently" would imply too much action. Hayricks and hay bales are stacked in some fields. The grains and the beans are still green. Harvest is a good way off. It's midsummer on the prairie—full of promise and grace and a little bit of danger, too. And in front of me, still the gravity of those mountains. Those real mountains of stone and wood and ice and fluid need.

9:45 A.M. 193 MILES WEST OF FARGO.

I cross the Missouri River at Bismarck.

One of the great many things I do not know is where most people believe the Midwest ends and the West begins. Perhaps no one has come up with a border that means anything. Political boundaries have nothing to do with the edges of a bioregion. Cultural psychology has oftentimes nothing to do with fact. As far as I'm concerned, however, on the northern plains the change from Midwest to West is the brown Missouri River. West of the Missouri River the land changes quickly. Hills rise into buttes. Rock piles dot farmland. The dominant color of the earth is brown now, not green. Every rise in the highway affords a view of miles and miles of buttes and arroyos, valleys, hills. The horses in the pastures this morning don't stand still here. They gallop and canter.

On the east side of the river, the stories are farm stories, weather stories, stories of large-scale immigration, community stories of harvest, famine, hope. On the west side of the river, the stories take on the names of leading characters. Custer. Sitting Bull. Lewis and Clark. Theodore Roosevelt.

10:10 A.M. 220 MILES WEST OF FARGO.

Approaching the town of New Salem, I'm sure the topic of conversation in every car, the only thing in the minds of those traveling alone, is one of the few things on this planet I wish would simply blow up. The cow.

The world's largest Holstein cow, the billboards say, a fiberglass monstrosity perched on a hillside. These kinds of icons have been celebrated all over the world, and yet the New Salem cow is, to me, perhaps the worst of them all. Not so much because it's a cow, but because it's huge and the land here has its own magic. Despite the change into a western light, the land here is still more flat than not, and you can see the cow from a very long distance. Almost like an auto accident that is grotesquely fascinating—no one can turn away from the hints of what might be possible in our own lives—as you're driving to or away from New Salem, you really can't look at anything other than the cow.

I've told many people many times that, if I were to ever go cow-tipping, this is the cow I'd go after. Take a chain saw; take off its two left legs, and watch the thing topple over. It worries me that I've said this so often, because if anybody ever does it, the police are going to come looking for me. I don't know why we want to put something like that in places like this.

The clouds this morning cast shadows on the hills that seem to race up one side and down the other, as if the shadows are enjoying their own kind of topographical roller coaster ride. The Jeep rises and falls, sways left and right. The act of forward motion is an act of joy on the western side of North Dakota; and, as I look forward to the Painted Canyon, to the Badlands, what I can't turn away from in my rearview mirror is the world's largest fiberglass Holstein cow.

There are time when you can pray for an appropriate lightning strike.

NOON. 314 MILES WEST OF FARGO.

If we can judge what we want by where we stop, by where we linger, by those places that afford, somehow, a moment of wonder, or peace, or a hint toward some larger definition of home and our own place in it, then the Painted Canyon is an essential place. For many people, *this* is what the Badlands look like: the canyon suddenly falling away from the prairie flatland, the reds and the greens and the browns, the coppers and the golds, all shining in the earth from the exposed hillsides, colored in layers like the walls of the Grand Canyon. Little bits of river down in the bottom meander around puddles left by last night's rain. It's the kind of sight that easily finds its way onto calendars and onto postcards. There is an awful lot of surface here. Acres and acres going up and down for every acre that goes left or right. What is it about seeing so much surface, so much topography, that always seems to capture our imagination? The buttes and the rises of the last couple hundred miles seem like mere hints as to what *this* can mean in terms of a physical beauty.

At the rest stop interpretive center, senior citizens, children, a group of bicyclists riding from Seattle to Washington, D.C., all stop, walk to the stone retaining wall, and gawk at the scenery. Everyone looking down as if the hole in the earth here—as if the canyon somehow pulled their eyesight. Nobody looks up. Nobody looks at the clouds or the sun breaking between them. Nobody comments about the wind or the sound of the birds—the crows, the killdeers, the sparrows. Everybody's captivated by what isn't, the earth that's missing, the hole that's created the Painted Canyon.

Cameras click right and left. People will remember this, I think.

Perhaps they will put their pictures of the Painted Canyon next to their pictures of White Cloud.

The parking lot here is filled with campers strapped into the beds of pickup trucks or towed. And it's a wonder that the people who leave them are going to walk the complete distance from their cars to the wooden fence or the rock retaining wall. Bermuda shorts, polyester jackets, office shoes or heels. Most of these people need a good diet plan.

This is the snob in me, I know. And it is entirely unfair, I know. Watching these people, however, I grow angry when it's clear no one actually wants to touch the Painted Canyon. No one wants to go hiking here. No one wants to feel the heat of their own body as they crest a hill and discover some grazing bison.

To get into the rest stop, you have to cross a cattle guard and pass a sign that says: "Buffalo are Dangerous—View from a Distance." And I wonder if these people believe it.

What is it we want from our landscapes? Is there a gravity to the sight of the earth? The cynic in me wants to shake the film out of the cameras here, to defeat the pin-in-the-map, slide-show mentality. But I'm also glad these people aren't down in the canyon, getting hurt, hurting what they see or fear. And when the cameras have caught enough, I notice a change in the people at the retaining wall. They affect a posture very much like one would have in church—quiet, slow-moving, staring for long times off into the distance the way one would consider statuary, an altar, a stained-glass window, or an idea. I doubt they are aware of this change themselves, even though I believe they are being spoken to.

And perhaps what draws people is, in fact, that openness, the fact that between here and the next rise in the Painted Canyon there is not so much dirt but so much perceivable space.

Unlike the others at the wall, the cyclists who have stopped here are without exception fit and strong. Their fine muscles would be the envy of most Olympians. They stop at a support truck, change to or from riding shoes. All of them smiling at the sight.

The cyclists are part of an organization called Bike Aid, working toward sustainable transportation. Every year they ride from the West Coast, from several starting points, to Washington, D.C. One of the men I stopped and talked with is from Australia. This is his first time in the States.

"What a lovely way to see the States," he said.

Even as they tease one young woman about the proper way to fall off a bicycle, I will admit I envy them—the slowness of a bike ride across the country, the ability to taste and touch and feel every bit of it, weather included.

A couple nights ago, up in the Beartooth Pass, they tell me, it snowed.

And I can feel the gravity of that sight and those mountains pull.

3:20 P.M. 480 WEST OF FARGO.

At a rest stop west of Miles City, Montana, I take a few minutes to stretch my legs and watch the clouds dance. For the past few hours I've been parallel to the Yellowstone River, the highway on a rise in the southern end of a valley. On the north side, a range of buttes, bluffs, cliffs. Very pleasant driving—the browns and golds of the hillsides, the greens and golds of the fields. The topography here, the way the land is shaped, calls attention from the highway. What's over there? I wonder. What's in that valley? What's around that bend? I think one of the attractions of this kind of landscape is that an answer seems so easily possible. You can't look at the sky and say, "What's over there?" because what's over there is just more changing sky—no body, no address, no place.

When you look at a range of hills, it's inevitable and natural to wonder what's on the other side. More dangerously, it's also possible to believe that where you are is somehow yours. This is my valley. That's your valley. But, for me at least, something there is that doesn't love a wall.

Gravity.

Gravity may be the weakest of the elemental forces, but there's no escaping it. Gravity is what will finally stop the outward rush of everything from the last big bang, and start the rush back home. Gravity holds us to the planet, holds the oceans into their place and the atmosphere to the globe.

And gravity, remember, plays a vital, that is, life-filled, role in the *behavior* of the universe. Gravity pulls us into valleys, over hilltops, around bends and rivers. Gravity is for humans pretty much the same thing as curiosity, or desire, or hope, or love. We want to know what we don't know. The mystery always needs to be solved. The mysterious, even if it's the face of God, always needs to be chased. Standing at the verge of the drop into the Painted Canyon and looking down, it's inevitable that we would feel the pull.

Watching the names of places go by on signs—Crown Butte, Grassy Butte, Sentinel Butte, Home on the Range—it's natural to wonder what stories rest behind the names. I should pull off at these places, get to know someone well enough to ask honest questions. Here at the rest stop overlooking the Yellowstone River, a stand of trees, green farmland, and then the browns of the buttes, it's impossible not to want to simply leave the car, walk down the hill, hike toward water.

Of course, there are also other reasons to want to leave the car and hike into the bush. As I leave the rest stop, local radio out of Miles City is having a brainteaser contest. The question: Which of the following is both a princess and a slave: Ada, Ophelia, or a few others? The answer: Ada, daughter of the king of Ethiopia enslaved by the Egyptians. The prize: a copy of the *Stepford Wives* video.

5:51 P.M. 600 MILES WEST OF FARGO.

In Billings earlier than scheduled, after a change from brown earth and buttes to forests of pine, aspen, spruce, and others I can't name, a landscape of green trees and bushes and grasses, then back to the same broad valley holding the highway and the Yellowstone River, I'm anxious for mountains. I'm anxious for that change, that *other* thing, the rise in the earth that, from my windows at home, I can imagine and need but not quite see. This land around Billings looks nothing, really, like the Red River Valley. But the change is not enough yet.

I stop at a hotel for a few minutes to check reservations farther on. A nice desk clerk brings me a phone and a phone book and gives me a map and helps me with directions.

The sky is once again a deep blue—clouds my field guide call *cirrus radiatus* and *altocumulus duplicatus*. The man on the radio says there may be more storms this evening. And all I can think about is how close I am to the mountains, and how invisible they still are.

A short while later, I turn off the interstate and join Route 212, heading toward Red Lodge. I'm told I'm less than an hour away. The signs here already read "Yellowstone Park," and yet I still can't see the mountains.

6:33 P.M. 636 MILES AWAY FROM FARGO.

Just south and west of the town of Boyd, I turn a bend in Highway 212, and a dark shape in the distance reveals itself slowly. There they are—the mountains rising in blue-gray from the green fields, the small hills, the rock outcrops I'm following now. Almost as if there is a border. I can't wait anymore. The mountains! My foot presses harder on the accelerator now. I find it difficult to look at anything other than the huge earth rising in front of me. And whatever desire for the earth I have in me says it's time to go meet it.

Day Two

RED LODGE—ELEVATION 5,555 FEET.
    Saturday morning.

10:00 A.M.

673 miles away from Fargo.

Checked into the Best Western last night. A friendly place with a desk clerk who is also a professional photographer, who has his pictures and slides with him at the desk, to show if you linger and chat. Pictures of mountains in sunshine, in rain, and in snow. Pictures of the sun over mountains. Pictures of the moon over mountains. And good advice about where to eat.

Finding the legs to walk on again after a day in the Jeep, I went over to Rock Creek, the narrow, rocky river that runs through town, shook out my fly line, and discovered a place to wade in. I'd been told the creek is two or three times its normal size right now, fast and rolling with runoff from the mountains. It seemed to be one continuous rapid from top to bottom. I waded in, in two or three places, tried my luck, and it didn't happen. No trout.

But that *other* thing was there last night. The size of the earth had changed, and my own proportion to it. It doesn't matter how many miles measure the distance, the mountains are the opposite of the prairie. Standing in the river, or walking in town, I could feel the simple weight of the earth around me in my breathing. Perhaps, I thought, with so much rock and dirt now above me as well, I actually weighed less here. Perhaps gravity pulled me ever so slightly in a new direction, sideways toward the cliff face, or up toward a summit. Not enough to be measured on any scale, but certainly enough to be noticed. And this change felt good.

Later in the evening, still looking for trout, I came upon another lodge with a bridge across the creek where I was told I could wade in. But the river was cascading over itself in whitecaps and boils here too. Beautiful to watch. Lethal to enter.

The lodge has a little stocked pond outside the front desk, and the clerk said I could try my luck there, which I did. Immediately after getting out my fly rod, a small crowd gathered. Other men and women brought out their fly rods, and pretty soon there were two and then three and then four of us casting into this small pond.

None of us caught anything, despite the trout rising and leaping, boiling the water on their own. These are educated fish—cast at daily, caught and released a hundred times by guests of the lodge. We all stood there, practicing our technique, embarrassed by bad casts, and not one of us caught a fish. Still wearing shorts even though the temperature was falling through the thirties, I finally left when my knees were shaking from the cold.

And as I was leaving, as I was talking with one of the men about what fly he was using, and bemoaning the fact that these were experienced fish, he said something fly fishermen often say to each other. "Yes," he said, "presentation is everything." And what he meant is the way the fly lands on the water, the way the fly line floats or doesn't, the way the fly moves if it sinks. If it doesn't look exactly like the bug it's trying to imitate, a trout will not go for it. But the phrase stuck with me for a different reason.

Presentation is everything. Isn't *that* what we want from our landscapes, for them to be *present?* To rise up and hit us hard? To not disappear into the mindless repetition of suburban lawns? To somehow force us into psychological reaction? To wake us from our sleep? To be that kind of gift?

Especially now, the morning of the second day of my trip, as the gray clouds have come back full and thick and steady rain falls on the town of Red Lodge, I'm wondering about presentation. I'm told the pass is probably open, but almost certainly it's snowing up there—and icy.

Presentation. What do we want from our landscapes? And what do we do when what we want is not what's delivered? The mountains are not supposed to be foreclosed by low clouds and rain. The mountains are not supposed to be cold in July. Instead, the stereotype says sunshine, dappled meadows of alpine flowers, waterfalls of brilliant-white airy foam, and not a single bug beyond the butterfly.

Frankly, I'm rather glad when the world works against what I can easily imagine or expect. But in the back of my head I heard the stories told by friends, prairie people like me, who had made this trip before me.

"You know," Cathy said, cups of coffee between us in her office, "I really wasn't sure if we were going to make it. And I don't mean just over the pass. I really wasn't sure if we were going to get out of there at all." She was telling me about driving over the pass in an unexpected snowstorm, her father at the wheel, when she was a little girl. She was telling me about the first time she realized her father couldn't really do everything, that he was human, and mortal, and what it felt like when the car began to slide and she saw that he, too, was scared.

"I'll never make that trip again." This comes another time, from another friend, Duane.

"Bad weather?" I ask.

"No. But I was driving this old boat of a Ford LTD. I couldn't see over the hood. All I saw was air and valley. I couldn't see the edge of the road, and there were no guardrails. I remember looking out the window at the switchbacks still going up, and thinking about how easily I could drive off the road. I was white-knuckled the whole time."

"Really?" asks Linda, the three of us standing in a corner of the college bookstore. "I've made that trip. And it was wonderful, really very beautiful. No problems at all."

"I'm looking forward to it," I offer.

"Never again," says Duane.

I had breakfast at the counter in a place called P. D. McKinney's, waiting for a promised clearing in the clouds, wanting to see, at least partially, the rise of the land and the space of the valleys. German sausage, two eggs over medium, toast, hash browns. The hash browns probably weighed three-quarters of a pound by themselves. The eggs were perfect and the sausage was spicy. A very pleasant morning.

But now, sitting here in the foothills of the Beartooth Mountains looking south and west out of town, I can see snow in the mountains. I can see the green hills rising up into the rocks, and even on this low morning I am drawn to that weight. I am sure there is something physical about the attraction of granite to flesh.

11:04 A.M. 675 MILES AWAY.

I begin the Beartooth Pass. A broad valley opens up into the Beartooth Mountains, misted this morning, shrouded in grays and blues of smoke and haze. The hills are forested in evergreen. Vertical rock is red and brown and almost white. People are out jogging this morning, walking even in the rain. A few cars come out of the valley—perhaps they have come over the pass—while a short line of cars motors in front of me as we all head into the mountains.

At the Exxon station, I asked the attendants if they'd heard anything about the pass. "I'm sure it's snowing up there," one of them said, "but you might break through the clouds. It'd be pretty nice up on top."

"Nobody's come down and complained too much," the other one said, smiling.

The highway is open. I'm driving down into a deep valley. This is fun.

11:15 A.M. 682 MILES AWAY.

The Custer National Forest. As far as I can tell, I've been driving downhill ever since leaving Red Lodge, which doesn't make sense. The mountains are getting taller and taller on both sides. The rock faces, each of them, and every corner I can't quite see around pull the eye, go up and sideways and around corners. A stream appears and then disappears. The trees get close, then provide a vista. The clouds lower, then open.

I wonder if the change in scale and perspective doesn't lead to a trick of the eye. I have felt that I have been driving downhill, but I pass Rock Creek every now and then, which is flowing back toward Red Lodge, and I know water has to run downhill.

My eyes tell me my Jeep should be coasting, that I should be worried about the brakes, but the Jeep won't accelerate. A small group of mule deer off in the jack pine watches me go by. I'm driving uphill. The way the mountains rise, it's just a trick of the eye to make me think otherwise. Rock Creek tumbles white against the green backdrop. It roars fast, the sound of it filling the air. The highway climbs into the mountains, the mountains climbing faster than the highway. Even in the clouds, what a drive!

I can see snow on the mountaintops. A quick look to my left, and I can see several layers of switchbacks going up the hillside, and my own laughter fills the Jeep. To the right, the valley and then sharp peaks, rounded domes, a full rising of the earth. Oh, what scenery! My God, Charles Kuralt was right! This is, without a doubt, the prettiest drive in America!

NOON. 694 MILES OUT.

I'm stopped at a scenic overlook—a short hike takes me away from the parking lot and up to an observation point. There are mountain goats here. And bighorn sheep. And pika, and rock squirrels, and marmots, and chipmunks. A sign tells me one bit of earth I'm seeing is named Line Creek Plateau, and another is named Hellroaring Plateau. I know there are stories, probably good stories, behind these names, but somehow I'm also sure the names will diminish the place. I don't have language for the way the mountains fall into valleys, for the way the rock becomes dirt becomes trees becomes water. I don't know how to explain the new rhythm of my heart in my chest when I sit and wonder about how much there is to imagine about what I see.

I've been playing leapfrog, stopping at pullouts to look, to make small hikes, and then drive on, with an older couple driving a Land Cruiser with Texas license plates. Here at the overlook, the woman gets out and turns to me—we're friends already, having smiled and waved at each other as we motor over the rising mountain—and says, her voice thick with the music of her accent, "Isn't this *something!*"

I agree with her. This is certainly something.

The rainfall turns to snow. I dig my raincoat out of my pack, hike around in shorts and a raincoat in the snow of the Beartooth Mountains.

12:30 P.M.

Above the tree line, where rain has turned completely over to snow—a fresh dusting covering the rocks and grasses—the road levels out a little bit. The more permanent snowfields, tinged with pink from an algae, are now as much below me in valleys and gullies as surrounding the roadside or resting thickly on the edges of small lakes. As I reach a plateau, the snow is falling in wet, heavy flakes.

12:45 P.M. I am now in Wyoming. The snow has become a snowstorm.

12:50 P.M. The snowstorm is worsening. The haze and the fog are closer and thicker. Visibility is much reduced. Guardrails have disappeared from the highway. Tall posts, deep enough for mountain snows, mark each side. A sign tells me that the gates may be locked and the highway may be closed suddenly and without warning in storms.

1:00 P.M. I'm tempted to put the Jeep in four-wheel drive just for my own peace of mind. Still going up. Once or twice I stop at small roadside pullouts and take pictures. This is near the top, I'm sure. A high, windy plateau. Small lakes in every depression. Snowfields. At one pullout, a father and son standing by their truck eat cold chicken and tell me they've just hiked up from a lower lake where they'd been camping. Both of them are tired, though smiling. They tell me they wanted to get out before the snow made them stay. I feel the pull of my own obligations, as well as the fact that I'm not prepared for much of a stay, and get back in the car.

1:18 P.M. A wall of snow to my left on the uphill side is about ten feet deep. Clearly, this road has been plowed recently.

1:20 P.M. A chairlift? A goddamned chairlift! On the downhill side of the road, the steel pillar supporting the cables. No one is here for sport today, but the thing is still there. Here. At the top of the Beartooth Pass, someone once stood here and wondered how the place could be *used*. As if simply being here wasn't, isn't, enough.

Just beyond the lift, a Sno-Cat with a snow blade parked on the side of the road.

1:21 P.M. That Sno-Cat may have been up at the summit. I am now definitely going downhill. The snow continues. Visibility increases and decreases as the mist and the haze get thicker and lighter. Snow still covers the fields on both sides of the car. When the haze lightens, though, I can see that there are tremendous valleys off to the left—large mountains out there somewhere.

1:24 P.M. Heading back uphill again. More snow walls border the highway. The one I'm passing now is probably eighteen feet tall. Names and dates are carved into the face of the wall. *Mark loves Jennifer. The Anderson's. Hi. Wow! June. July.*

1:26 P.M. At a little pullout, I pass a sign that says, "The Bear's Tooth" with the sign pointing off, and all I see are mist and snow. Visibility is two-tenths of a mile. Cars on my downhill side appear suddenly, headlights shining. The drivers are not smiling.

2:35 P.M. 714 MILES OUT.

I am where Beartooth Creek runs into Beartooth Lake and where I've just spent an hour or so in drizzle as well as downpour rain, chasing rainbow trout—and winning. Coming down out of the height of the pass, nearly eleven thousand feet above sea level, the snow made me wonder if I'd be trapped for a very long time, and then disappeared into rain. At a log cabin store, the "Top of the World Store," I bought fresh hot coffee and a fishing license for Wyoming—asked directions for a place, anyplace, I could find water and mountains and strong fish. Directions to this campsite, this small marsh where river becomes lake, were given happily. A beautiful setting of a green mountain with patches of snow at the slopes, thick forests of evergreen.

What is it we want from our landscapes? What is it that pulls us to them? Standing at the end of the Beartooth Creek flowing fast into the lake, rolling over boulders under willows and pines, what do I get here that's different from the prairie? It can't be just the change in scenery that's important. Why is the peace I feel here, the fundamental relaxation of my spirit, so much different from the peace I feel in my own home with my family?

There is a great deal I don't know. But I suspect something about all this. I suspect what we desire from the shape of the earth is a hint that we still don't know the whole story. Casting for these trout, I find myself glad for the snowstorm in the pass. I have a new story to tell now, a story no one will expect. And, casting for these trout, in the shadow of these beautiful mountains, I suspect I'll have these stories with me when I get back home. Each walk on the flat prairie, itself wonderful and large, now holding mountain storms just over the visible horizon.

2:55 P.M.

The sign says, "Cattle on highway," and, indeed, there are.

3:21 P.M. 741 MILES OUT.

Yellowstone National Park. Northeast entrance, elevation 7,325 feet.

I've been passing through a burned-over area, part of the big Yellowstone fires of a few years ago. Lodgepole pines on both sides of the road, little more than vertical charcoal, though the brush underneath them is deep, living green. Still descending. I'm not sure where they've all come from, but the road is now filled with motorcycles, sedans, every type of car you can imagine—the going made slow because of pickup trucks pulling campers.

A bison on the side of the road. The animal is just lying in the grass, quietly chewing on something, facing the road—almost as if the Park Service had said, "Sit here for a while—we need a photo opportunity." The cars all slow down to take a picture, and then, after fifteen or twenty seconds, off they go. In each car, a camera holds another slide, another trophy. And I wonder if anyone knows, or remembers, last winter, when the bison were shot by the hundreds when they left the park to find food, by ranchers as well as by Montana state officials, because some people were afraid the bison would infect beef cattle with brucellosis.

What is it we want from our landscapes? Can "Saw a buffalo" be enough of a story?

4:07 P.M. 769 MILES AWAY FROM FARGO.

Tower Junction, 6,278 feet above sea level.

It's a long drive through the north end of Yellowstone. Every turnout is filled with eight to ten cars. Every possible pulling-off place filled with two or three. Everybody taking pictures. As I sit at the Tower Junction, in front of Roosevelt Lodge, I see twenty or more people on a trail ride. They're all on horses, but none of them are really riding. Most of them look petrified. Still, the horses have been doing this for a long, long time. What are these people looking for?

4:53 P.M. 788 MILES OUT.

I pull off the road, the perpetual parking lot at Yellowstone, to visit the brink of the upper falls in the canyon, and I don't even get out of my Jeep. The lines going up and down the walkway are tremendous. There is something to be said for viewing nature, and there is something to be said about viewing it alone. There's an old phrase: if you love wilderness, stay out of it. It's selfish of me to wish everybody else was gone. I'm sure they wish I was gone, but it doesn't deny the fact that there are too many people here. License plates from Ohio, Georgia, Tennessee, Idaho, Montana, Wyoming, Minnesota, North Dakota, Texas, Utah, British Columbia, Virginia, Colorado, Turtle Mountain.

What do we want from our landscapes? At the Artist's Point overlooking the Grand Canyon of Yellowstone, people are smiling, happy, laughing, patting each other on the back, almost saying, "Wasn't that something?" And yet that something is available because of a manicured, paved trail to a point overlooking the canyon. Nobody's hiking here; nobody's getting off into the canyon itself. Is it enough to see it, enough to have only the visual? Is it enough to get to a place like this so easily? To not get out and hike, to not get out and touch the mountain?

I'm tired, I know. And ill-tempered by the press of people, the ease of being here, the consumerism of a photo-op visit to a national park. And yes, I *know* I'm trying to get through the park as fast as I can. I know I'm no noble guide here. I have a long way to go before I sleep tonight. Other mountains. But if this was where I was stopping, then by golly I'd want to get my boots dirty. What stories do these people tell each other when the day has faded into starlight? How close the coyote came to the car? How they could smell the sulfur-cauldron area even with the air-conditioning on?

Gravity. What do we want from the shape, the rise and fall of the earth to our feet? What calls to us, any of us? In the mountains I thought I'd had a beginning of an answer. Here, it's all a mess again.

6:10 P.M. 829 MILES FROM FARGO.

The Continental Divide, elevation 7,988 feet.

6:48 P.M. 857 MILES OUT.

Jackson Lake to the west, and beyond it the Grand Teton Mountains—really very pretty, even though they're shrouded and gray in mist. Finally making some speed on the road. Through the rain, it's risky to look over my shoulder at the mountains. With the rain, the forests look more like a tropical rain forest than anything else. It's lush and green, and water spills from narrows in the hills at every turn.

The clouds close in again. Valleys in the clouds reveal valleys in the mountains, however. The steel gray of the clouds giving way to the reflected steel-gray snowfields, the lake reflecting it all. The greens and dark blues of the forest and grasses on the mountains. Twilight is coming on—even this early. I pass nearly twenty cars, all pulled over to the side of the road to watch a moose frolic in a marsh.

What do we want from our landscapes? What kind of gravity calls us away from the places we collect our mail—and what are we really looking for? For me, at least, I'm wondering if this valley might be one possible answer. Broad and flat, filled with sage and willows, its aspect is very much like the prairie I love at home. There's open ground, good space to move, or run, or dance. But, and here's the change, the scene is framed. All four sides of this valley reveal visible mountains.

At home, I can see forever. But a foot is as perceivable as a light-year if there's no border. Here, in this valley, I can see less far—but I can know what I see. So you tell me: What do we want from the shape of the planet? Do we feel the tight closure of a steep canyon more intimately than the breadth of a summit view? Or is shape finally not the issue at all? What kind of gravity pulls us from home to home? Could it be we're just looking for the Other, for hints toward awe, toward a better articulation of the mysterious? I'll admit I really don't know.

Yet, south of Jackson, tight by a new river and heading once again into the mountains, I'm already wishing for unframed sky.

A TOURIST'S PETITION

THIS ONE BEGINS ON AUGUST 17, ON THE MINNESOTA SIDE OF THE
Red River of the North, around four o'clock in the middle of a hot
and humid afternoon, while fishing. Before this day, I had never
cast a line into the Red River, despite having crossed it daily for
years. Before this day, I had dangled my feet in its waters, cross-
country skied it when frozen and snow covered, walked long
stretches during each season to simply enjoy the fluid aspect of
water and wood in the course of a year. But I had never really
rested on its banks. Always, I was the one in motion, the river and
the woods a landscape I passed through. On this day, after a morning and noontime filled with reading, I rested and let the landscape
of my home move past me.

Not two weeks before this hot August afternoon I had been in
the western Arctic, fishing mountain streams for salmon, char,
trout, pike, grayling. I had been fishing with people too, the travelers I met, asking what took them so far from home, what desire in
their hearts put them on roads they knew in advance could prove
dangerous and certainly expensive. I was hoping to learn something, some small truth about the unarticulated values that moti-
vate our living.

Wilderness calls to many people deeply. And there is a desire, I believe in each of us, to discover whatever rests where the roads finally run out. I had seen on a map the road leading farthest north, and its pull was personal, intimate, as seductive as the wink of a lover. So I hit the road, as had the others I'd met, to discover something about the world and our own small place in it.

Why is it that each of us will stop, gladly, to hear a road story? Why is it that, if a friend of mine begins a story with *I was driving out of town yesterday and* . . . , I know I've been made a promise? I know the long or short story to follow will recount some adventure, some unexpected turn in the day's chronology, and I know it will evoke some sympathy in me since I've made that trip, or similar trips, myself. My friend's story, no matter how simple or mundane, will broaden my knowledge and understanding of what is possible, and hearing the story I will offer my friend a type of confirmation—in the way that a secret really isn't a secret until it's shared.

Road stories, by definition, it seems, promise some small glimpse of what lies over the horizon, both physically and metaphysically, and we just can't get enough of them. Chaucer's *Canterbury Tales* is framed as a collection of road stories. William Least Heat Moon's *Blue Highways* is a collection of road stories as well. The Christian Nativity begins with a road trip, and there's a travel section in our Sunday newspaper.

And why is it that road stories almost always create a large or small desire to get on the road oneself? In the comfort of our offices or living rooms, a cup of coffee in one hand and a newspaper or journal or travel book in the other, the word pictures of mountains, deserts, parliament houses, tent cities, ancient rituals, personal disaster and triumph again bring us the news of what we cannot see from our own domain, places and things made exotic by virtue of existing outside the everyday routine.

Back from traveling myself, still unclear what to say about what I'd seen and heard and felt in the Arctic, I looked at my rod and reel, both gathering dust, and decided it was time I fished in local waters, cast a line down deep where I cannot see, hoping all the while that my skill and patience would bring something home.

The Red River is less than a five-minute walk from my home, though each is invisible to the other. The walk takes me through one community park, past another, in front and along the sides of the homes of my friends and colleagues and people I've never met. This August afternoon was steamy, and by the time I reached the river, a civic bicycle path leading me to the shore behind the Moorhead power plant, sweat already trickled down my face and made my exposed arms and legs shine. I decided to settle on a concrete shelf, part of a pump house that used to supply water to the power plant before there was concern that doing so warmed the river too much. Because I'd heard of the fish that used to get into the system there, I figured this was as good a place as any. In front of me, the river was glassy and bright. Small wind ripples sometimes traveled the river's surface, but mostly the afternoon was still.

A fisherman does not settle into the act of fishing immediately. Just as long-distance road trips find some rhythm of their own after the first few hours have passed, just as dinner parties wait for that gathering of friends in the kitchen before anyone believes the evening is up and running, the first cast of rod and reel simply confirms that the equipment is working. The second says something about a rusty arm or an imperfect aim. Maybe the third cast is when fishing begins. Maybe the thirteenth. In any case, there comes a time when the action of casting and reeling, the ancient motions memorized by the arm and hand, becomes invisible, and the mind takes up other issues.

I say this essay began that August afternoon because on this day I was troubled by an idea I could not express. When I was on the road, I missed my home and family deeply. I called home every day, as is my habit when traveling, and each new sight or insight I discovered was taken in and added to a context that finds its foundation in my living room, in the act of watching my children play, in the thousand ways my wife and I say I Love You without speaking the words. On the telephone, my wife would tell me about her day, the accomplishments of our children, and I would tell her about the mountains, the moose and caribou and bears I'd seen, the rivers where I'd gone fishing with some success, the people I'd met, and the stories I'd heard. In the quiet seconds between her stories and my own, the distance between us became intimate and painful.

Yet, now back in Moorhead, I had been taken over with wanderlust. Casting my fishing line into the Red River, I was filled with a desire for the Klondike River, or any of a dozen clear and tumbling Arctic mountain streams where I had performed this identical ritual. At home, I desired what many people call Nature. Visiting Nature, I desired the routines and comforts of Home.

Fishing from the concrete shell of the old pump house, I watched as one and then another brown pelican flew past me, each of them not more than twenty feet over the water, following the river's course from north to south. I watched as a snowy egret landed on the river's western banks and picked its way among the driftwood and mud. Fish I did not catch jumped after insects I could not see. Not five minutes from home, in the middle of a small city, the routines of nature were as obvious as the pump house, the power plant, the bank building, and the apartments I could see from my own resting place.

So where was I? In Nature or at Home? Why had I so often left one in my attempts to discover the other? If both Nature and Home exist in the same place, must one obscure the other? Certainly, our contemporary discourse implies a division between Community and Nature. Television news spells out the debates between owls and lumber, between fish and hydroelectric dams. Each issue of *Audubon, Natural History,* or *Nature Conservancy* holds pleas for preservation against an encroaching suburbia. In our mailboxes, the Wilderness Society, World Wildlife Fund, and Cousteau Society compete for our spare dollars with mail-order catalogs, political campaigns, and the Cheese of the Month Club.

And we are the heirs of an established tradition. The American Essay, from its very beginnings, seems to create a divorce. For example, this is Henry David Thoreau, the opening to his essay "Walking":

> I wish to speak a word for Nature, for absolute freedom and wildness, as contrasted with a freedom and culture merely civil,—to regard man as an inhabitant, or a part and parcel of Nature, rather than a member of society. I wish to make an extreme statement, if so I may make an emphatic one, for there are enough champions of civilization: the minister and the school-committee and every one of you will take care of that.

"Walking" is not his best-known work, of course—*Walden* holds that honor—but I believe it has a special power to it nonetheless. Coming at the end of his life, "Walking" has the force of summation, of conclusion-making to its words and images. These are the ideas his life had tested and found worth keeping. "Walking," like *Walden,* holds a foundational place in the history of American writing about Nature, and Thoreau is telling each of us to get out of the house and out of the town.

> I have met with but one or two persons in the course of my life who understood the art of Walking, that is, of taking walks,—who had a genius, so to speak, for sauntering: which word is beautifully derived "from idle people who roved about the country, in the Middle Ages, and asked charity, under pretense of going à la Sainte Terre," to the Holy Land, till the children exclaimed, "there goes a Saint-Terrer," a Santerer, a Holy-Lander. They who never go to the Holy Land in their walks, as they pretend, are indeed mere idlers and vagabonds; but they who do go there are saunterers in the good sense, such as I mean. Some, however, would derive the word from sans terre, without land or a home, which, therefore, in the good sense, will mean, having no particular home,

but equally at home everywhere. For this is the secret of successful sauntering. He who sits still in a house all the time may be the greatest vagrant of all; but the saunterer, in the good sense, is no more vagrant than the meandering river, which is all the while sedulously seeking the shortest course to the sea. But I prefer the first, which, indeed, is the most probable derivation. For every walk is a sort of crusade, preached by some Peter the Hermit in us, to go forth and reconquer this Holy Land from the hands of the Infidels.

Clearly, Thoreau is teasing. But this is also definition-making. This is the building of an intellectual or philosophical or perhaps spiritual foundation to give purpose and meaning to a nonutilitarian relationship with the natural world.

Sauntering is not a word we use often these days. The meanings of words change, for better as well as for worse, and today *sauntering* seems to imply a type of laziness. As a matter of fact, I do not think we have any good word for sauntering these days. Walking is something we do for exercise, for utility. Strolling is an opportunity for lovers or friends to talk out-of-doors. Sauntering has even fallen out of favor as a habit of mind in an age more given to told facts and neat statistical graphics on a television screen than the joy of a discovered truth.

If we have a word that *celebrates* destinationless wanderings on foot through the course of an afternoon or day, a word that offers praise to the men and women who open their days to other rhythms, I cannot find it.

We do have a contemporary word for sauntering, though it is often used with such a negative meaning that I am almost afraid to bring it up. Certainly, its current usage implies nothing about the celebration of an open eye and mind. Those of us who travel far enough from home are transformed, suddenly, into (ack!)— Tourists. And if Thoreau wants to speak a word for Nature, for absolute freedom and wildness, this day I want to speak a word for the Tourist, for the circular motion of the tour, for the act of leaving and the act of coming home, for exploration as well as closure.

To go, and be filled with home. To be at home, and be filled with the desire to wander. Is this a contradiction, some type of permanent desire to be somewhere other than where we are, a dissatisfaction rooted somewhere deep in each of us? Or is this a desire to expand our personal and spiritual geographies?

A philosopher or a pessimist would say we are simply dissatisfied, still caught up in some existential malaise inherent in the postindustrial society. For example, Erich Fromm, in *Man for Himself*, says:

> Self-awareness, reason, and imagination have disrupted the "harmony" which characterizes animal existence. Their emergence has made man into an anomaly, into the freak of the universe. He is part of nature, subject to her physical laws and unable to change them, yet he transcends the rest of nature. He is set apart while being a part; he is homeless, yet chained to the home he shares with all creatures. Cast into this world at an accidental place and time, he is forced out of it, again accidentally. Being aware of himself, he realizes his powerlessness and the limitations of his existence.

Yet, quite simply, I believe Fromm, and others like him, are wrong. Since at least the 1970s, Barry Commoner, Greenpeace, Love Canal, Three Mile Island, Chernobyl, Rachel Carson, and the humbling photographs of Earthrise taken by Apollo astronauts have taught and reminded us that we live on only one planet, that we are all each other's neighbor. If we have a desire to travel, to see what lies over whatever horizon is revealed to our own histories, inherent in that desire is also the desire to return home, to bring the road songs back.

I should not claim, by the way, that this is a new idea. Before Thoreau, there was Emerson, in whose first book, *Nature*, we read:

The greatest delight which the fields and woods minister, is the suggestion of an occult relation between man and the vegetable. I am not alone and unacknowledged. They nod to me, and I to them. The waving of the boughs in the storm, is new to me and old. It takes me by surprise, and yet is not unknown. Its effect is like that of a higher thought or a better emotion coming over me, when I deemed I was thinking justly or doing right.

One hundred and fifty years later, Barry Lopez, one of our time's most eloquent and lucid nature writers, rediscovers this same idea. In his book *Arctic Dreams*, he writes:

I took to bowing on these evening walks. I would bow slightly with my hands in my pockets, toward the birds and evidence of life in their nests—because of their fecundity, unexpected in this remote region, and because of the serene arctic light that came down over the land like breath, like breathing.

. . . As I traveled, I came to believe that people's desires and aspirations were as much a part of the land as the wind, solitary animals, and the bright fields of stone and tundra. And, too, that the land itself existed quite apart from these.

The physical landscape is baffling in its ability to transcend whatever we would make of it. It is subtle in its expression as turns of the mind, and larger than our grasp; and yet it is still knowable. The mind, full of curiosity and analysis, disassembles a landscape and then reassembles the pieces—the nod of a flower, the color of the night sky, the murmur of an animal—trying to fathom its geography. At the same time the mind is trying to find its place within the land, to discover a way to dispel its own sense of estrangement.

But is leaving home the only way? Are our lives somehow restrained and clouded by the communities we build? American nature writing often implies there is some type of greater value to be found in the wilderness or at the frontier. Those of us with the itch to travel read the narratives and descriptions of life on the road with a certain very real envy. But to assume that there is a greater value away from home than at home is, I think, a dangerous mistake. Listen, for example, to Scott Russell Sanders, from his book *Staying Put:*

> One's native ground is the place where, since before you had words for such knowledge, you have known the smells, the seasons, the birds and beasts, the human voices, the houses, the ways of working, the lay of the land, and the quality of light. It is the landscape you learn before you retreat inside the illusion of your skin. You may love the place if you flourished there, or hate the place if you suffered there. But love it or hate it, you cannot shake free. Even if you move to the antipodes, even if you become intimate with new landscapes, you still bear the impression of that first ground.
>
> . . . Like sap in maples, the urge to mend the house rises in me with special force in spring. So it happens that I am often hauling supplies up the front steps while birds in our yard are gathering twigs and grass and leaves. As I stagger to the door with a clutch of two-by-fours on my shoulder, I see catbirds or cardinals or robins laboring to their nests with loaded beaks. Whenever I stop sawing or drilling, I am likely to hear a chatter of construction from the trees. The link between their labor and mine is neither whimsical nor quaint, but a matter of life and death. The river that carries us along is wild, and we must caulk our boats to keep afloat.

Other writers now are taking up the life of the community, its natural rhythms and currents and patterns, and making it cause for celebration as well. After *Blue Highways,* a book that celebrates a voyage out, William Least Heat Moon wrote *PrairyErth,* a book that celebrates the voyage inward, the life of a single Kansas county. Kathleen Norris's *Dakota* celebrates the life of what she calls, aptly,

I think, a spiritual geography. Likewise, Minnesota author Paul Gruchow, in his essay "Eight Variations on the Idea of Failure," writes:

> To plant a garden is to enter the continuum of time. Each seed carries in its genome the history that will propel it into the future, and in planting it, we ourselves stretch one of the long threads of our culture into tomorrow.
>
> A home, like a garden, exists as much in time as in space. A home is the place in the present where one's past and one's future come together. It is the crossroads between history and heaven.

Writing about Nature. Writing about Home. Writing about Nature as a part of our own community, our own communities. Nature as something we share a responsibility for, as inherent in whatever definition of home or town or regions we may use. If our understanding of the world and each other is to develop at all, then we must be working toward a type of peace with the things we share.

If I have a personal hope in all of this, it is that someday we will all be Tourists. I do not mean to say that every one of us will in some fashion need to visit the places on our personal maps still labeled *Terra Incognita,* camera straps slung over our necks. Rather, it is my hope that we will recognize that coming home after a day at work is, in its essence, the same thing as walking a wilderness road for the very first time. When I go home this evening, the light will have changed. Mail will have arrived. My wife and children will have stories to share from their days, just as I will have stories to share about my own. Dust will have settled into some corners, or will have been cleaned. In short, my home will be as fresh this evening as any part of the world will ever be to my limited ways of seeing. I will be a Tourist at home, as I am a Tourist everywhere else on this planet. And I wish to speak a word for the Tourist.

Coming home provides the context for our road songs, just as the road provides the context for our stories about home. Both provide the foundation for our souls. And just as real fishing does not begin with the first or second cast of rod and reel, Tourism, in the good sense I want to mean today, does not begin with the first outbound airplane ticket, or the second. Each day creates a new *Terra Incognita* out of the whole universe, each morning a new and unexplored venue for the Tourist. To be a Tourist in the way I mean is to learn a way of seeing freshness, a way to value even the smallest and most perfunctory actions of our days. As the world grows more populated and therefore more problematic, it is in the little excursions as much as in the large ones, in the small observations as well as the grand ones, that we will discover ourselves, that we can make an honest connection with others, that we can remind each other what it means to belong to each other, that we can establish a peace before politics. If anything, Tourists are storytellers. And stories are how we love.

Like any good Tourist, I have the desire to return where I started. Not to the Red River of the North, but to the idea that made me go there, to the words and ideas of Thoreau, who takes the opportunity himself to echo Shakespeare:

> My desire for knowledge is intermittent, but my desire to bathe my head in atmospheres unknown to my feet is perennial and constant. The highest that we can attain to is not Knowledge, but Sympathy with Intelligence. I do not know that this higher knowledge amounts to anything more definite than a novel and grand surprise on a sudden revelation of the insufficiency of all that we called Knowledge before,— a discovery that there are more things in heaven and earth than are dreamed of in our philosophy.

Every one of us is a Tourist. In the silence of reading as well as in the joy of excursion. Wherever you are right now, how could you know what words would come next? How the paper would feel in your hands? How your chair would be arranged? How the light would reflect from the walls and the faces of people near you?

We do not expect our own stories, or who we would hear them with. Look up for a moment. Isn't there as much Wonder, as much material for Story, for Community, and for Peace, in your room, as there is anywhere else, everywhere else, on the planet?

BANFF IN A DAY

1

THIS IS NOT A GOOD IDEA.

Ten minutes after six o'clock in the morning on a Wednesday, October 14, and I'm pulling out of my neighborhood to see if I can make it from Moorhead, Minnesota, to Banff, Alberta, in a single day. A thousand miles, or more. The odometer in my seventeen-year-old soft-top Jeep reads 107,555.8 miles accomplished successfully. I have a full tank of gas, and the tires are young. The engine leaks oil.

How far can you go, in just one day? How far away is a one-day's drive? It all has to do with limits, with looking at a map and saying *this far.* It all has to do with the borders of home. As far as I can tell, Banff is an eighteen-hour drive from here, maybe twenty. And this, you see, is why I'm up so early, and why I could not sleep well last night. If I can get there in a day, I think, I can still call it home.

On the wall of my daughter's bedroom there is a large map of North America. And if I put my hand up to it, I can spread my fingers to join the places I've driven in a day. With my little finger on

Moorhead, or Fargo, my thumb reaches Kansas City easily. Columbia, Jefferson City, Osage Beach, Camdenton, Missouri, require a little stretch. Chicago is an easy spread. South Bend and Indianapolis are just beyond my reach, but close enough to include. Casper, Wyoming, is a full hand, but possible. In Canada, Winnipeg is just the length of my index finger. Saskatoon is thumb and middle finger made into an L. Regina is the tip of my thumb to the end of my palm—no fingers needed. Toward Banff, however, my hand can't even come close. Thumb on Fargo, my little finger, hurting, can only make it to Swift Current or Maple Creek in Saskatchewan. Beyond those, Banff is the whole length of nearly two index fingers, placed end to end.

I think I can make it to Banff before sleep tonight, but I am not certain. Half an hour ago I turned on my computer and looked at the radar screens, scanned the weather between here and there. All clear, I think. A fine day ahead.

Of course, this trip has an official reason, though this reason is as unimportant as usual. I'm going to the annual conference of the Western Literature Association. I'm going to try to push the magazine I edit to the scholars and students there. I'm going to stand behind a little desk in some convention-space lobby, and wait for people to walk up. With luck, they will pick up a copy of the magazine, and if they ask I will answer their questions.

It's a good conference, I'm told, and a good journal. But I could just as easily slip this morning into the fuselage of some jet, whose interior will be remarkable only in that I will be unable to tell it apart from every other jet in the sky, and I could walk up and down jet ways and through customs and into taxicabs and then this way and *oh, look at that quick!* then that way toward the intimacy of a convention center that can accommodate thousands.

There is the official reason, and then there is the reason that matters. Road trips, when chosen, are heart songs. To see the sun come up on the prairie this October morning, to see the landscape change from prairie to Badlands to mountains. To see fall light, sunrise then midday then twilight, catch fire on horizons my imagination is not yet large enough to detail, and to smell the wind off trails I've never walked. This is the reason for a long day's drive. To know what's home.

This trip, like all good trips, begins in darkness. Not only the actual darkness of this late fall day—the sun won't be up for another hour—but a kind of personal darkness as well. I've seen the landscape between here and Rugby, North Dakota, here and the customs offices at Portal, here and Saskatoon, here and Edmonton. But I've never seen any of it at this time of year. And, more important, I've never seen the world near Banff. I've never seen towns named Moose Jaw or Medicine Hat. I've never seen the way the wind will move the grasses and crops up there, and I've never heard the way a human voice can sound at home, there.

There are ways to be in love with where you live, and there are ways to be in love with the things you have not seen.

At 6:10 this morning, Moorhead is asleep. There is only one other car on the road with me. The traffic lights blink on and off, red and green, as if practicing for the rush hour that's two hours away. Back at home the alarm is going off. Maureen is getting the kids up, first Kate, then Andrew, and starting to get them ready for the bus. Clothes on, cereal and juice, teeth brushed, then coats and backpacks slipped over shoulders. The bus comes early for our two kids—seven o'clock—and every morning requires a new ballet of encouragement and threat.

It's a cold morning, somewhere in the forties. Clear sky. The stars are bright overhead. Even though it's still too dark to see this well, the trees here in town still hold their autumn colors. The oaks and the cottonwoods and the poplars and the elms have turned their yellows and reds, though the birches seem to have already had their time. It's the kind of day where you really do think about pumpkins and Halloween, about playing outside in just a warmer jacket, about finding wood for the fireplace in the evening. It is not yet the kind of day where you think about winter, about snow and blizzards. Still, if you live in Minnesota, or North Dakota, you develop an ear for Canadian weather, for the sheer speed of the storm, for the suddenness of clear, hard cold. One, two, maybe three good snowstorms have already passed by us to the north, and I'll be driving into that landscape.

This trip is not a good idea, or at least the part about trying to do it in one day is not a good idea. Maureen is worried. Other people I've told have shaken their heads as if I've lost my mind, and a Canadian friend who knows this route well simply looked at me, smiled, then said, "Well, you can always stop."

Banff in a day. Yesterday I got the car gassed and oiled and everything checked. I've got an overstuffed bag, a new pair of boots, and a meeting to get to.

2

6:20 IN THE MORNING. A strong cup of coffee from home, a 1983 Jeep CJ-7, and I'm on my way westward. Already, there is a little more traffic on the road. The town is waking up. Men and women sip their own cups of coffee at the traffic lights. Soon there will be work, and noise, congregation and community and commotion. But for now there is an odd sort of morning peace. Not even a hint of something in the sky that would resemble daylight yet, but still there is this sense of where you are, of being in place, of moving through rhythms and expectations that rise from the land or fall from the sky.

As the Jeep comes up to highway speed, I cross the Red River of the North, then just a few minutes later the Sheyenne River. Heading west through Cass County, I am reminded that there are many ways for the prairie to be beautiful, and one of them is in the middle of the night. Moonglow on fields, small grains or beets or snow, or even just the silhouette of trees against stars on new-moon nights. Farm lights in the distance—the whites and oranges and golds of house and barn lights, yard lights. Northern lights, aurora borealis, waves and sheets of yellow and indigo and gold. Thunderstorms a good way off, or far too close.

Both the Red River and the Sheyenne at night are just dark paths leading north and south and then around a bend, quick glimpses from the highway. But it's impossible to cross them and not think of history, not think of the stories both rivers provoke.

On the radio this morning I learn that today is the anniversary of the day Chuck Yaeger first broke the sound barrier. Today is the day Martin Luther King Jr. received the Nobel Peace Prize. Today is the day the Beatles finished working on the White Album. These stories are large, important, international. But they are really just the summaries of a thousand more local stories that led to the larger conclusions. Even if they don't remember, most people in this country have heard of the Red River, its flooding in 1997, the tremendous fight with sandbags to save people's homes and lives. We made the news in New York, and London, and Christchurch. And perhaps this point is too obvious to mention now, but no one who wasn't here during that time knows any real story about this place. As is true for everywhere, and every story, if you didn't touch it, you just don't know.

There is something we love about motion and speed. There is something we love about going faster—not, of course, about getting anywhere, but just the act of travel, the act of rocketing through space. This worries me, and excites me greatly. Every mile away from home is a mile away from a story I can say, honestly, I know how to tell. And every new road sign, every new conversation, every new place-name, is the opening of a story I still get to learn.

7:30 IN THE MORNING; 107,637.5 on the odometer. The Continental Divide at 1,490 feet. Sunlight is just beginning to fill in the spaces from darkness now. There are clouds in the East. This is not one of the prairie's most spectacular sunrises.

The harvest in North Dakota is pretty much over, except for the sugar beets. Back in Moorhead, a constant stream of trucks muddies the roads as the beets are pulled from the ground and rushed to storage. Timing is critical. The beets need to be pulled when the root temperature is in the fifties, and sugar is at least 17 percent. Yet they need to stay in the ground until the air is cold enough. Sugar beets are stored outside, and if the air gets too warm, they rot. Even in hard winter, when the air is ten or twenty degrees below zero, the temperature in the middle of an unventilated beet pile can reach twenty degrees or more. So when the air gets cold, the race is on. And this is a local story.

This morning, however, already far enough west to have left the beets, I am reminded nonetheless how agriculture affects the way we look at the landscape. In the springtime: young crops, pale-green stalks rising out of black earth, every day measurable and rich, a promise in the process of being fulfilled. In the summertime: mature crops, wheat and barley and soybeans and sunflowers and corn, almost nostalgic in their familiarity and warmth, confirmation of a common definition of home. And in the fall there is the dance of combine and harvester, of swathing and lifting, the gatherings and holidays.

Then comes winter. When the crops are gone, our perception of the land changes. Our relationship with what we're looking at has an emotionally different center. I don't know what this feeling is, really. It's not a sadness. It's not a loss as much as it is a good signal that it's time to stop playing—bad weather is coming. On the prairie, spring and summer and autumn landscapes each hold a picture of human hope. After harvest, however, and throughout each winter, the land speaks differently.

Ten minutes before eight o'clock, 107,655 on the odometer, I'm passing through Jamestown, and the light is getting brighter. It's now morning in North Dakota. Coming into town, I passed the signs for the tourist attractions including White Cloud, the albino buffalo, a sacred animal to many Native American people. As I passed on the right the area where the buffalo herd is kept, White

Cloud looked at first like a boulder sitting out in the field. Then the boulder took on buffalo shape. The rest of the herd, as usual, I'm told, stood apart from White Cloud. Too different to be included. And it makes me wonder if the sacred must always also be the lonely.

At the exit, the augers at the implement store are lined up nicely. At the McDonald's, when I tell the lady at the intercom that a second order of hash browns sounds good, she comes back cheerily, "Sounds good to me, too!" At the gas station, the clerk is friendly and helpful.

The elm trees and the poplars and oaks that I pass here in town have still got their leaves. It's not winter yet. It's simply a cold fall morning after harvest.

This is perhaps not a good sign; but, just west of Jamestown, I pass highway department trucks—highway department *salt* trucks. The plows aren't on the front ends yet, but this is another sure sign that things are changing. As I pass water in fields and ponds and ditches, I see that the edges are frozen.

3

NORTH OF BISMARCK on Highway 83, the sunshine comes and it's clear I'm entering a different kind of terrain. To the east, the flatland prairie. To the west, the wide valley of the Missouri River. And beyond the river, buttes and valleys. The gentle rises in the fields to the east become angular and sharp to the west. To the east, the land is planting-green. To the west, the land is grazing-brown. The horizon to the east is as flat and as shimmering as the horizon at sea. The line to the west has landmarks and breaks. For the eye, at least, the West begins at the Missouri River.

According to the National Weather Service in Grand Forks, North Dakota, the eye is not the only indication. Based on 1961 to 1990 data, western North Dakota receives annual precipitation of 13.5 inches in the north, and 16.1 inches in the south. Central North

Dakota receives 16.5 inches in the north, and 18.5 inches in the south. Eastern North Dakota receives 18.5 inches in the north, and 21.5 inches in the south. Of course, I am heading north, and west.

White clouds, steel-blue clouds, and blue sky over green and brown, gold and red hills. It's 9:45 in the morning and the odometer reads 107,777.7. I'm passing fields here of sunflowers, unharvested and brown, their heads drooping and heavy.

There is a sign on the side of the highway advising farmers not to mow the grass here, not to collect it for hay. The thin ribbon of grass that borders the roadway is wildlife habitat, and protected. I've seen sparrows and barn swallows, hawks and geese and gulls and ducks and crows this morning, and I haven't really been looking.

This is historic ground, too. Nearly two centuries ago, also in mid-October, Meriwether Lewis and William Clark and the Corps of Discovery entered North Dakota, traveling the Missouri River north, and west. In his journal, Clark reports that migratory birds appeared like "black clouds flying." In his journal, Lewis writes that, "Our hunters killed ten deer and a goat [big horned sheep] today. Great numbers of buffalo swimming the river. Large gangs of wolves follow the herds. The country is fine, with high hills at a distance with gradual assents, the timber confined to the bottomlands."

Lewis and Clark were heading for the Mandan villages, which were certainly not the wilderness. More people lived there then than lived in St. Louis, or Washington, D.C. Fort Mandan became their home for the winter. This is where they met Charbonneau and Sacagawea. This is where they prepared to leave what they already knew.

If the Mandan villages were the largest "city" on the plains two hundred years ago, perhaps it should not be surprising that shortly after I pass the sign for the Lewis and Clark Interpretive Center at sixty-five miles an hour I come up on the Cold Creek Station—North Dakota's largest power plant. I've been able to see this in the distance for what feels like twenty miles. A bluish, smoke-producing monster. Brown buildings, two tall gray smokestacks, white bands at the top, cooling towers, conveyor belts. Power lines, of course. Everywhere around here are power lines.

Just north of the power company, a large overland conveyor belt crosses the highway. White steel surrounds the trough, protects the coal as well as the passing cars and trucks, and the belt never stops moving. As you speed by on the rush of gasoline, you can watch the coal shuttle from the Fall Creek Mining Company land to the power plant. And remember, the sides of the highway here are wildlife habitat.

10:25 in the morning. 107,818 miles and counting. Lake Saka-kawea and Lake Audubon, a road that splits the two. The water is gray this morning. Gray, and gunmetal blue. There is no wind to speak of. The water is not quite glassy, but it's certainly calm.

4

IF I CAN GET THERE in a day, I think, I can still call it home. But is this claim a good idea? Prairie geography and weather. Red River Valley floods. Even Lewis and Clark. Because this is where I live, these are my stories. These are the stories I tell if someone asks me where I'm from. But stories make claims both ways. If I am going to say the whole of a day's drive is my home, then the stories in that circle, *all* the stories in that circle, claim me as much as I claim them. Some of the stories are wonderful, thrilling, and noble. Some of them are not.

10:30 A.M., 107,824 on the meter, and I pass a missile silo on the east side of the road. Chain-link fence, metal hatches, white ventilation pipe, it looks like nearly every other missile silo I've ever seen—unobtrusive, almost invisible, and profoundly unsettling. This is the planting we don't talk about much. An old story goes that if North Dakota were to leave the Union, it would become the third-largest nuclear power in the world, just behind the rest of the

United States and Russia. I've never checked the numbers, but the story sounds right.

This morning, at silo number D-4, a solitary truck idles near the chain-link fence. A workman (a soldier?) tinkers at a box. I cannot tell you if D-4 still has a missile in it, or if this is one of the decommissioned tubes. But a short while later the highway brings me past another silo, and then another. Just outside of Minot, I see that the missile squadron participates in the "adopt-a-highway" program.

These are the contradictions of any good home and its stories. I am certain that the men and women from the Minot Air Base who pick up trash along the highway and train to end the world are wonderful people. We all have our blessings and our faults. North Dakota is a haven for refugees from Bosnia, Somalia, and elsewhere. Yet the state is often seen as intolerant. North Dakota is the beneficiary of government programs far larger than the state's small population would warrant alone, and the state is home to some fierce antitax history and bloodshed. In my part of the world people still often sleep with their home doors unlocked. Yet we have thieves and killers here, too.

If I am going to claim this place as part of my home, then I must accept the dark places as well as the light.

West of Minot, Highway 52 travels through one long, low valley—hills on either side rising to a kind of plateau. Today, hayricks decorate the harvested fields. At a small intersection I see a street sign—394th Street. I'm still a ways out of town, but not so far my location can't be numbered, planned for, traced. There is a rail line in this valley, grain elevators every now and then, cattle, and the occasional horse.

The rocks in the hillsides here have been arranged and then whitewashed so that they spell out numbers. 76. 84. 98. High school classes? There is a 97 and a 96 and then a 95. A 77 and an 88. Suddenly they're all over the place.

I wonder about putting these on the hillsides. I've seen towns where clock faces are put in the hillsides, artwork of various sorts marking the land. These numbers on the hillsides are evidence of—what? Under 63 it says, "State Champs." Next to 65 it says, "State Champs." Off in the distance around a small reservoir, I can see 55. This tradition has been going on for some time.

At the Kenmare Amoco Station, in the Dakota Convenience Store, a place that advertises the "cleanest restrooms around," I order chicken strips, french fries, what seems like several pounds of candy, and a soda. I learn from the gentleman working the desk that the rocks in the hills are from the Kenmare High School, and they date back to 1949—not a single year has been missed. They used to give the students a couple days off—called them "rock days"—to do the numbers, but the man tells me one year some students got hurt, not badly, but the activity became a liability issue for the school. So, now, the students do it after school. The rocks are all placed on private farmland. As the man says, it really is a testament to the kids around here that they have to do it on their own. There is nobody helping them, and they get it done every year.

The Amoco station is a gravel-driveway kind of place, a little concrete around the pumps. Inside, a little convenience store and coffee shop. Very attractive, actually. Although this place is small, and rural, and tucked away in an arid corner of a state most people can't find on a map, the people and the very rocks in the hills tell stories of pride and history.

West of the town of Bowbells, of course, I begin to pass the missile silos again.

5

Canada!

One o'clock. 107,967 on the odometer, and I am in Canada. Here at the border, in a town named Portal, they actually searched my car! Normally, for me at least, passing into Canada is a brief stop at a drive-up window. A flash tells me some machine is taking a picture—of me, the Jeep, the license plate number, whatever. A stern-looking man or woman asks me why I'm wanting into Canada, where I'm going, what I'll be doing there, if I have any weapons, any contraband. The answers are all simple enough. Today, though, I think I came around that last corner a bit fast. Today, though, I think the customs officials wanted to ease a bit of the need for speed out of my right leg and foot. They didn't find anything, of course.

North of Portal now and heading for Moose Jaw. Sunshine on the northern prairie. The clouds have all disappeared except toward the eastern horizon. Away we go! Same sun. Same taste to the air. But this is a new country now. The stories have changed even if the shape of the earth has not. Maybe twelve hours left.

Outside the town of Midale there is a white grain elevator with a gold Pool logo on the side. A small galaxy of birds too far away from me to know what kind sits on the steep pitch of the grain elevator's roof. I'm not near enough to cause it, but suddenly it appears as if there is a waterfall—hundreds of birds falling off the roof all the way down to within inches of the ground before their wings spread and they soar off to land a short distance from where they started. I can't tell if they're having fun, but the sudden grace is beautiful.

Two o'clock in the afternoon—108,007 on the odometer—and the clouds are closing in. I don't think there's bad weather ahead, but the clouds are thickening. I'm pulling out of the McDonald's at Weyburn where I'd stopped for coffee and to talk to my wife on the telephone. I saw a Jeep Cherokee pull in with Minnesota license plates. The driver saw my license plates, waved at me. I waved at him. We both smiled.

Why? Because neither of us is local here? Because neither of us has a full inventory of the local stories? Because here we are both more ignorant than not? Or did we smile at each other because here, in this place away from where we are most intimately knowledgeable and known, we saw on each other's car a symbol of something, a story, perhaps a kind of singing, we share? And didn't we also recognize the new story we are writing—the story of our new travels?

Each of us carries a part of a gargantuan story. A small part, to be sure. But nonetheless complicated or rich because of its individuality. And we often find ourselves in chorus.

So perhaps, then, coming back up to highway speed, it's not surprising that what comes to me is an old bit of Bruce Chatwin's *Songlines:*

> He went on to explain how each totemic ancestor, while traveling through the Country, was thought to have scattered a trail of words and musical notes along the line of his footprints, and how these Dreamingtracks lay over the land as "ways" of communication between the most far-flung tribes.
>
> "A song," he said, "was both map and direction-finder. Providing you knew the song, you could always find your way across country."
>
> "And would a man on 'Walkabout' always be traveling down one of these Songlines?"
>
> "In the old days, yes," he agreed. "Nowadays, they go by train or car."

Yet it begins to bother me that such ease toward community, the fast, sweet friendship that can be made on only the basis of a shared license plate homeland, can obscure what is honest, and real, and local. You see, there comes a point in the middle of every long-distance road trip when a routine is established. I've been passing dirt road after dirt road, semi after semi, railway crews one after the other reconstructing the line that runs next to the highway here. Every so often, a small town comes along, the speed limit goes down. I pass an elevator, the speed limit goes back up. All of the fields have been harvested. The vegetation in the ditches along the highway is red and gold and green and brown. Silver grain bins stand out in fields. The world moves by faster than a mile a minute, and it all looks very much the same.

At this speed, you get some sense of size, some sense of how big the Great Plains are, how much there is to grow. You get some sense, too, of these small towns—each of them unique and yet each of them instantly like the other. As they go by you get some sense of how urgent they are. It would be easy, at this speed, to mistake one song, one Dreamingtrack, for another.

Coming up on the town of Lang. Now there's an elevator, a water tower, a Quonset hut, a railway line. The road curves here for a moment, then straightens out. The houses are white and brown and gray. Some John Deere tractors sit in the fields. Some are very old. One looks somewhat new. There are satellite dishes in occasional yards, a red barn with white trim, a man and his son working on a snowmobile, another barn, and then it's gone. The Saskatchewan Pool Elevator is the last thing before the town fades away.

4:25 at the town of Caron, 108,139 on the odometer. There's snow on a distant hill and in the ditches along Highway 1. It's clearly the end of October. Geese spiral down out of the sky, up from the wetlands and farm ponds here. The afternoon is turning gray. Westbound on the Trans-Canada Highway heading for Banff.

At the Shell station in Moose Jaw, a guy driving a Jeep much newer than my own pulls up.

"You're a long way from home, eh?" he said.

"Not really," I said.

"Are you hunting?" he asked.

"Nope," I said. "Just visiting."

6

4:45 IN THE AFTERNOON. 108,165 on the odometer. The sun appears in a thin span of clear sky above the horizon yet below a sky full with thick dark-blue clouds. I'm passing a hill completely capped in snow. The ditches and the fields, the low spots, are all snow covered now.

There is very little traffic this afternoon, even here on Highway 1, the Trans-Canada. No towns in the distance—just the highway, the power lines, the occasional other car, the onset of snow, and the gathering clouds. All of it fresh, and beautiful, and unique. I've never been here before. I have no history here, no story sitting before any turn of the road. And what we cannot expect has *presence* when it appears. We cannot defend against it, and so it enters us, hard or softly.

4:55 and the snow cover is no longer just that one hilltop. The ground around me on both sides of the highway and in the median is snow covered. Stubble perforates the snow in the fields, but that's the exception now instead of the rule.

A few days ago I asked a friend who lives in Alaska if she had any snow yet. She said no snow, but heavy frost and more moose than she was used to seeing. A sure sign of a close winter, and perhaps a hard one too. Here in western Saskatchewan, in the rolling hills of the prairie, there's snow in mid-October. It's time for winter, and I'm suddenly glad I brought my snow boots, my gloves, my vest, and my hat.

What is the quality of a landscape that makes us call it beautiful? I do not believe it is only the dramatic towers or cliffs of a mountain range, or the ungraspable breadth of an ocean or prairie horizon. There is, I think, in what we call beauty a sense of mystery. In landscape, at least, a sense of largeness. Of openness. Of possibilities we have yet to imagine. Of real borders being much farther away than only what we can see. There is a sense that what makes this place beautiful begins a long way away, or a long time ago. Just beyond the town of Chaplin, a lake, large enough that one eyeful cannot find each corner, set between some hills. And the hills themselves, unforested, unoccupied, covered with either the brown of dormant grasses or the white of new snowfall.

A sign tells me that I'm passing the Western Hemisphere Shore-bird Reserve. And although I don't know it yet, what I am passing is impressive. What I see this day from my Jeep is a landscape I call beautiful, the lake and the hills and the snow, the openness of it all, the huge sky. And I certainly wonder what the stories here may be. Months from now, however, at my desk and computer, a cup of strong coffee in my hand while a Minnesota blizzard makes seeing the end of my own driveway impossible, I will look at my notes and type the phrase *Western Hemisphere Shorebird Reserve* as a search term. What I uncover is tremendous.

The reserve is actually a network of reserves, from Tierra del Fuego to the high Arctic. This network, a collaboration of govern-ments and conservation groups and landowners and individuals, has one purpose: to maintain and promote the health of the fly-ways and the migratory corridors. According to the Environment Canada website, "As of March 2001, the network of over 165 orga-nizations includes 46 officially recognized sites in 7 countries, stretching from Tierra del Fuego to Alaska, protecting an estimated 10 million hectares of habitat and 30 million shorebirds."

The network began at the Bay of Fundy. On May 29, 1997, how-ever, Chaplin, Old Wives, and Reed Lakes became western Canada's first hemispheric shorebird reserve, covering 43,000 hectares. Again according to Environment Canada, "This area pro-vides annual habitat for more than 200,000 shorebirds including over 55,000 Sanderlings or one-quarter to one-half of the west coast South American wintering population and over 200,000 Stilt Sand-pipers. In addition, up to 200 endangered Piping Plovers, which is 15% of Saskatchewan's population, and almost 4% of the North American population inhabit the area."

Another website, this one for the reserve network itself, gives me a list of birds seen at Chaplin. American avocet. Baird's sand-piper. Black-bellied plover. Buff-breasted sandpiper. Dunlin. Hud-sonian godwit. Killdeer. Least sandpiper. Lesser golden plover. Lesser yellowlegs. Long-billed curlew. Long-billed dowitcher.

Marbled godwit. Pectoral sandpiper. Piping plover. Red knot. Red-necked phalarope. Ruddy turnstone. Sanderling. Semipalmated plover. Semipalmated sandpiper. Short-billed dowitcher. Spotted sandpiper. Stilt sandpiper. Upland sandpiper. White-rumped sandpiper. Willet. Wilson's phalarope.

I even learn that Chaplin Lake is saline, and mined for sodium sulphate. And I learn that the mining can help the birds.

I do not know any of this, however, as I drive by, admiring the way the afternoon sunlight lights this land and the surface of the pretty lake. All I am really wondering is if I can still call this landscape home. Doesn't home imply history, an ownership of at least one good story set in a particular place? My only claim is that I am here, that it is possible for me to get here in a day, and my desire to listen to what stories I can find. Does learning the story of the reserve network after the fact count? How can it not, combined with the story of the road trip itself?

Five o'clock in the afternoon and the town of Swift Current ninety kilometers ahead. As I pass by the town of Morse, another large lovely lake. The snow is mostly gone away now, though still hiding in the pockets of ditches and shadowed hills. There is bright sunshine, too, as the clouds have thinned. Red grain elevators, or silver, with the Pool logo. An Esso station, with geese.

Five hundred kilometers to Calgary. Six, maybe seven, hours left.

7

8:15 IN THE EVENING. 108,363 on the odometer. It's been a long, quiet, golden afternoon in western Saskatchewan and now eastern Alberta. There is just enough light left in the sky that the grain elevators, tall trees, and some buildings are silhouetted against the western horizon. There's a Bach harpsichord concerto on the radio. The town of Medicine Hat just straight ahead.

It's almost warm enough to forget my jean jacket. At gas stations and pullouts, people are friendly. And I wish I had language for the kind of peace this is. I've seen so much land today, so much space. The land here is very much like the land where this day began. I'm still on the prairie, still on what is called the Plains Grassland. I know the seasons here, the look of the sky, the taste of the incessant wind. Not too far in front of me, though, the Rocky Mountains. Not too far in front of me, a different way of seeing the earth.

So what is the true border of what we can call our home? From my own experience, I know nothing about the people here. My own experience is just this one day on the road. But home, in its best and most hopeful definition, is a great deal more than just one person's experience. When we use the word *home*, we talk about family, about friends, about classmates and colleagues and people who know us. Their histories, and their stories, are part of my understanding of home, just as my history and my stories fill some corner of theirs.

I'm trying to work this out because as I travel the narrowed highway from Gull Lake through Tompkins and then into Walsh, I do know a history, though it's not my own. Eleanor Coomber, a friend of mine, is a Canadian. Her father, Al McKinnon, is from this part of the world.

"Burt Hargrave," she said. "Burt and Amy Hargrave. They were friends of my father. They had this very old and huge house, right at the Alberta border. He was six foot five, and she was six foot two, or close to that. Really fascinating people, and he was very handsome. Everyone knew Burt and Amy. And everyone knew they were home on Sunday afternoons and evenings. People would just gather there naturally. Burt once hosted a reunion of his World War Two company or regiment or whatever, and hundreds of people came, even way out there. The way my dad tells it, Burt was quite a character. He once told my dad that if a horse didn't have the right expression on its face, he wouldn't ride it that day. Another time, when the weather forecast was for a tremendous blizzard, Burt said it wouldn't happen. When bad weather's coming, he said, the cows all move into that hollow. The cows weren't worried, so neither was Burt. And they were right, too."

I never met Burt or Amy Hargrave. But I do know Eleanor, and I've met her father more than once. I do not know the stories here as much as I know the people who do. Is that enough to make the claim? Is this any different, really, than sitting down with a distant, though blood, relative, and sharing the expanse of a songline? At roadside pullouts I read signs about the bonanza farming boom and bust here, about the oil industry boom and bust here too. The history and civics lessons are interesting, but nowhere near as real or as telling as Burt Hargrave's examination of a horse's face. That story, that understanding, is enough, I think, to say yes—in some small but important way, this is still home territory.

Coming around a corner, I see the city lights of Medicine Hat. And as I pass through town, I get to see the world's tallest tepee. White wood or metal—no fabric or skin around it. Just the structure itself, a bit stylized at the top and the middle for support. Also in Medicine Hat, although it's too dark for me to see it, the South Saskatchewan River.

8

9:10 AT NIGHT. 108,411 on the odometer. The sun has set. It's dark except for a faint glow in the western horizon, silhouetting some of the clouds.

At night the Trans-Canada Highway becomes like any road at night, a river of asphalt pavement, striped lines in the middle, on the left and on the right. The dark black of patched places. It's difficult to see anything to the left or the right, although overhead there are stars. More here, it seems, than there are at home, although I know that's not true. Farm lights are not very common here. Headlights of oncoming cars illuminate the other half of the road. Always in the distance, it seems, there is at least one radio tower—the glowing and the flashing red lights—evidence that for either love or profit we are always talking, always listening.

11:40 P.M. 108,550 on the odometer. Calgary, Alberta. I am nearly asleep at the wheel as I pull into town. I pass the sites of the Olympic Games, the ski jump, and arenas. The stories I know here are only the most generic.

At a gas station, the light doesn't work in the bathroom. They've got a plunger set by the door, so you can put the stick in to prevent the door from closing and let a little hallway light come in. The clerk and a friend who's come to visit think this is extremely funny. And for some reason, I do too. In the middle of the night, it makes perfect sense.

Once again, gas, fresh coffee, hard candy, and the road.

9

AT THE BANFF CENTRE, in Banff, Alberta.

I cannot tell you what time I got here last night. I did not remember to write down the odometer reading. West of Calgary, fog joined the darkness, and the only thing I could see was the roadway a short distance in front of my Jeep. I did not see the mountains appear. I did not see the river I know from maps runs next to the road. At the entrance to the Banff National Park there is a booth, where I suppose information and maps and advice are handed over to excited tourists. The lights were on when I got there, but no one was working. I proceeded on.

Tired as I was, I barely remember finding the hotel, parking, checking in, carrying my bag to the room, getting in bed. This morning, though, as I walked out of the hotel lobby's front door, I damn near kissed an elk before I realized what was standing in front of me. The elk here move right through the campus of the convention center. It's not unusual to walk out a door and find one munching on some grass or some leaves.

This morning the clouds have not lifted, and we've already had nearly eight inches of snow.

So the question still remains. As I stand here this morning, cup of good coffee in hand, surrounded by the Rocky Mountains, elk so close I have to be careful, new snow gathering on my shoulders and hat, can I use the same word here—*home*—that I would use more than a thousand miles to the east, where the land is flat and snow is some weeks off? I have no stories here. I own no part of this history. But there are people here this morning who expect me. Friends and colleagues who have come to this conference for their own reasons. We have breakfast plans, and lunch plans. Plans to go hiking and plans to sit still. We have plans to learn this place as best we can in a few days.

And although I don't know it yet this morning, I will meet an old friend here—a man named Bob I knew in graduate school in Massachusetts. There was a strong group of us in those days: friends and lovers and classmates. We would sometimes gather in Bob's apartment to dance, to drink, often to embarrass ourselves, and always to tell stories. Those stories, and those memories, are as good a definition of home as any building. When I see Bob later today there will be hugs and oh-my-Gods, and we will find a space to talk, to get caught up with each other and with what news of our friends we may have.

And in a few days, when the meetings are over, and I point the Jeep eastward, to drive again the roads that brought me here, I will leave with new stories and old friendships made stronger. I will feel as if I'm leaving one kind of home.

So perhaps this is the best I can offer. This is not my home because I can get here—in a day, or in a week, or in a lifetime. But because I can get here, I can begin to make this place, its stories and its landscape, a part of my home.

THE LOLO PASS

The trip over the Bitterroot Mountains via the Lolo Trail was perhaps the severest test of the whole expedition. Winter was already beginning in the high country in September, and the party would struggle through deepening snow. Lack of game forced them to kill and eat some of their horses. Pack animals slipped and fell down steep mountainsides. . . . The long and difficult trip from mountain pass to meadows dashed all hope of a short portage across the Rocky Mountains and ended dreams of an easy passage to the Orient.

—Introduction to volume 5 of *The Journals of the Lewis and Clark Expedition*, edited by Gary Moulton

1

Some frost this morning every Man except one, out hunting, a young man Came from the upper Village & informed me that Capt Lewis would join me abt. 12 oClock to day. one man killed a Small Sammon, and the Indians gave me another which afforded us a Sleight brackfast.

—William Clark, August 27th Tuesday, 1805

2

MONDAY MORNING in Missoula, Montana. Nine o'clock and the sun is just beginning to rise into a clear sky. There is snow on southern peaks, fog in the valley, and frost on the windshields. I've hauled my bag from the warmth of a hotel room and plunked it in the back of the Jeep, though I've not yet had the courage to start the engine. This is a morning to watch, I think. A morning to watch the sun fill a valley in the mountains with autumn light.

Driving across the prairie, especially when you're leaving, is an exercise in freedom. You leave what you know—the flatness of the prairie, the crops, the people, the ways of seeing what's important and what's not—and you move into other landscapes, into other territories. What you know may or may not be true. There are clouds on the prairie that tell me if it will rain or snow or turn to tornado. Those clouds don't mean the same things in the mountains. Yesterday, I drove from Moorhead to Missoula, past the North Dakota Badlands, up onto the foothills of the Rockies, and then into the Rockies themselves—the landscape changing from prairie farms and grasslands to buttes and then to mountains.

There's something about coming up into the mountains when you live on the prairie that also invokes a fear. Ice on the bridge, the sign says. You don't know in October if ice on the bridge means now or later. A spin here isn't just a dump into a ditch. A spin here can fall you a thousand feet or more. And in the mountains, the horizon seems impossibly close. You just can't see that far anymore, and you worry about what may be both invisible and close.

3

Set out at 7 a.m. this morning and proceeded down the Flathead river leaving it on our left, the country in the valley of this river is generally a prarie and from five to 6 miles wide the growth is almost altogether pine principally of the long-leafed kind, with some spruce and a kind of furr resembleing the scotch furr. near the wartercourses we find a small proportion of the narrow leafed cottonwood some redwood honeysuckle and rosebushes form the scant proportion of underbrush to be seen. at 12 we halted on a small branch which falls in to the river on the E. side, where we breakfasted on a scant proportion of meat which had reserved from the hunt of yesterday added to three geese which one of our hunters killed this morning.

—Meriwether Lewis, Monday September 9th, 1805

4

EVERY ROAD in yesterday's trip, and even now as I cross the Bitterroot River, brought signs that this path is history. "The Lewis and Clark Trail." And it is impossible to not think about the Corps of Discovery. North and west of the Mandan villages, every day was fresh, and original, and dangerous, and hard in its beauty and threats. Four times in the darkness last night I crossed the Clark Fork River.

Driving in the mountains at night is both sad and instructive. Sad because you can't see anything—only the ridgelines and summits outlined because there are stars where the mountains are not. Otherwise darkness, the occasional farm light, the occasional railway signal. Instructive because the ribbon of the interstate remains alive and bright—this great mindless thing called commerce. Lewis and Clark, after all, were sent to discover a route for trade.

On the CB radio, the truckers talk about DUIs being felonies in Canada, then about the bad repair of a road in Louisiana. Thinking about the mountains ahead of me, I press the talk button on my own radio and ask a question because I think they might know: what is the highest drivable pass in the continental United States? Silence for fifteen or twenty seconds and then a chorus of "I don't know, but I wouldn't want to be caught there."

Coming into Missoula last night in the darkness, I found the hotel and a comfortable bed. This morning as I leave town I am amazed by something I've seen before, but every time, every time, it does wonders for the heart. The hills here are forests of evergreen and birch and aspen. The birch and aspen and poplar are all bright gold, and the rivers I pass are steaming in the early morning cool. October in the mountains!

5

[A] fair morning Set out early and proceeded on thro a plain as yesterday down the valley Crossed a large Scattering Creek on which Cotton trees grew at 1-1/2 miles, a Small one at 10 miles, both from the right, the main river at 15 miles & Encamped on a large Creek from the left which we call Travelers rest Creek. killed 4 deer & 4 Ducks & 3 prarie fowls. day fair Wind N.W.

—William Clark, September 9th Monday, 1805

6

THIS MORNING I am driving south, out of Missoula, first into the town of Lolo, then a turn to pick up Route 12. I'll follow the Lewis and Clark route up over the mountains. On the Idaho side, I am supposed to meet Peter Chilson and Ron McFarland, two friends driving up from Moscow, Idaho, and Pullman, Washington. Our plan is to spend this day chasing trout, and then drive back to town to work for tomorrow and the next.

In Lolo, at an intersection, the streets are named Glacier Drive and Ridgeway Drive.

I am supposed to meet Peter and Ron at a campground called Jerry Johnson up in the hills, on the other side of the Lolo Pass. Oddly, nobody in Missoula seems to know where that is. It's on the other side of the pass, they all tell me, as if everything they don't know must be there, on the other side of the pass.

Lewis and Clark stopped, every time they could, to meet with natives, to learn what they could about the land and its stories, to hear what would come next, over the pass, around the bend. A few miles up from town, there is a sign for Travelers' Rest, where Lewis and Clark spent five days preparing to cross the mountains. They were not, of course, the first people to do so. There were the people who discovered the trail, and then those who made the trail a habit. When the roadways came in, there were the people who surveyed, who scraped the earth, and then pressed it back down, and those who poured the asphalt. There were hours and days and months of work, and then centuries of practice and revision, to make my transit at seventy miles an hour possible. Logging trucks and tourists roll through these hills and over this pass every day, each of us stopping at restaurants and hotels to talk about the shape of the earth. How could anyone here not know what is over the pass?

Nonetheless. The sky could not be prettier this morning. East-facing mountains, snow covered, literally light up, reflect sunlight off the ice like diamonds. It's a cliché, I know, but it's true.

7

. . . and the third remained, having agreed to continue with us as a guide, and to introduce us to his relations whom he informed us were numerous and resided in the plain below the mountains on the Columbia river, from whence he said the water was good and capable of being navigated to the see. . . . [H]e said it would require five sleeps wich is six days travel, to reach his relations.

—Meriwether Lewis, Tuesday September 10th, 1805

8

9:30 IN THE MORNING and I've made my first mistake. I was told back in Missoula that Highway 93 becomes Route 12. Well, I saw the signs for 93 and settled in for the drive. In the town of Florence, I discover I'm nine miles past the turnoff for Route 12. I'm heading back—worried about being late for Peter and Ron.

Highway 12 is just a two-lane road. There is a four-board fence on the right now, much like those bordering farms near Charlottesville, Virginia, home to both Jefferson and Lewis—horses in a meadow, bright-gold trees, the hills sit in front of me, a pair of joggers, a man and a woman, on the south side of the road. There is frost on the ground here this morning, magpies at the roadside.

Just a few miles past the intersection, I'm already in a deep valley, steeply pitched walls on either side, and a small stream to my left. A pair of knee boots would suffice for crossing today. When the valley opens up a bit, I can see Lolo Peak to my left.

There are places already where Route 12 slows to forty miles an hour and the road twists fast to the left and right. The valley closes up. The golds and the greens in the trees intermix almost one-on-one. There are horses and cows in the pastureland here. Some homes here clearly account for some money, and some homes here clearly don't. I pass a brick entrance to a driveway with a locked gate, an old railway car put in place to act as a bridge, a Lewis and Clark campground.

This is not a ridge-top drive. This is not the Beartooth Pass with its switchback vistas or the Dempster Highway in the Arctic where you can see for a hemisphere. This is canyon driving. Around one corner and you're blinded by sunlight, and around another corner you're plunged into darkness. Lolo Creek is fifteen to twenty feet across, strewn with boulders and rocks. It's a calendar stream for trout fishing. The only other traffic is semis going downhill hauling logs.

I have that old optical illusion again. I would swear from looking at the road that I am driving downhill. Yet, if that were true, the stream would be flowing uphill and the mountains would be falling away instead of rising toward a pass.

9

The road through this hilley Countrey is verry bad passing over hills & tho' Steep hollows, over falling timber &c. &c. continued on & passed Some most intolerable road on the sides of the Steep Stoney mountains, which might be avoided by keeping up the Creek which is thickly covered with under groth & falling timber Crossed a mountain 8 miles with out water & encamped on a hill Side on the Creek after Decending a long Steep mountain.

—William Clark, September 12th Thursday, 1805

10

A ROADSIDE POINT OF INTEREST tells me about Lewis and Clark—Soldiers as Naturalists. One section of the sign reads:

Along Lolo Creek and over the Bitterroot Mountains, Lewis and Clark recorded several animals they'd never seen before—ruffed grouse, spruce grouse, mourning dove, Steller's jay, and the broad-tailed hummingbird. On this section of the trail, some of the plants they recorded included grand fir, subalpine fir, western larch, Englemann spruce, white bark pine, lodge pole pine, mountain lady-slipper, common snowberry, and western huckleberry.

The sign also tells me that

Jefferson's letter of instruction admonished Lewis and Clark to bring home scientific, anthropological, and geological information: "Your observations are to be taken with great pains and accuracy, to be entered distinctly and intelligibly for others as well as for yourself. Several copies of these, as well as your other notes, should be made at leisure times and put into the care of the most trustworthy of your attendants to guard by multiplying them against the accidental losses to which they will be exposed."

In this meadow, the sign tells me, the Lewis and Clark expedition camped on September 12, 1805.

Animals I've seen on this trip so far: deer, antelope, skunk, magpie, grouse, eagle, sparrow, raven, crow, cow, sheep, horse, and a world of swift brown or bright flashes heading for cover, too fast for my eye.

11

I proceeded on with the partey up the Creek at 2 miles passed Several Springs which I observed the Deer Elk &c. had made roads to, and below one of the Indians had made a whole to bathe, I tasted this water and found it hot & not bad tasted The last in further examonation I found this water nearly boiling hot at the places it Spouted from the rocks (which a hard corse Grit, and of great size the rocks on the Side of the Mountain of the Same texture) I put my finger in the water, at first could not bare it in a Second—as Several roads led from these Springs in different derections, my Guide took a wrong road and took us out of our rout 3 miles through intolerable rout, after falling into the right road I proceeded on thro tolerabl rout for abt. 4 or 5 miles and halted to let our horses graze as well as waite for Capt Lewis who has not yet Come up.

—William Clark, September 13th Wednesday [Friday], 1805

12

PASSING THE LOLO HOT SPRINGS what I see is a "Resort and Eatery." *Resort* in the loosest sense of the term. Muddy parking lot. Rusted pickup trucks. A sign that says "Welcome Hunters." In the steep hills on both sides of the roadway, the larches have turned bright gold.

Three miles from the Idaho border and there's snow on the evergreens. My ears are popping, and I keep slowing down despite a heavy foot on the gas. I must be climbing. I must be near the top of the pass.

Welcome to Idaho and the Pacific time zone! Six percent grade going down for the next several miles. A truck turnout place to check brakes. Yee ha, I think. Here we go!

Just over the pass the valley opens up, and I can see miles and miles of snowcapped peaks—brown and gold and green forest. Very different from the prairie. The sign says, "Winding road next 77 miles." I love it.

13

Several horses Sliped and roled down Steep hills which hurt them verry much The one which Carried my desk & Small trunk Turned over & roled down a mountain for 40 yards & lodged against a tree, broke the Desk the horse escaped and appeared but little hurt Some others verry much hurt, from this point I observed a range of high mountains Covered with Snow from S E. to S W with Their top bald or void of timber.
—William Clark, Wednesday [Sunday] Septr. 15th, 1805

14

AN INTERPRETIVE SIGN at the Lolo Trail crossing reads: "When Lewis and Clark came up this ridge, June 29, 1806, they ran into a shower of rain with hail, thunder, and lightning that lasted about an hour. But they got out of deep Lolo Trail snow after they reached Rocky Point and descended to Crooked Fork below this turnoff. They reported then that they ascended a very steep acclivity of a mountain about two miles, crossing this highway here to reach their old trail to Lolo Pass."

There is a map that shows the state of Idaho, and the Highway 12 marker, and underneath the Highway 12 is the phrase, "Oh, my!"

15

Checkerboard legacy. Many changes have occurred since the time Lewis and Clark used this route in the early 1800s. The mountains you see around you are now shared by the US Forest Service and the Plum Creek Timber Company. Each owns alternate sections of land creating a checkerboard pattern. This pattern of ownership began here in 1908 when the US government granted the Northern Pacific Railroad Company alternate sections along the proposed railroad route. As you travel across Lolo Pass, you will see a variety of textures and openings on the landscape. They represent natural fire patterns and timber management practices on private timberlands and the national forests.

I am in the Clearwater National Forest.

Coming down out of the pass I can see that a small summit, not the top of the mountain but a ridge top or a mound, is on fire. The air is filled with the smell of wood smoke.

"Watch for falling rock next 60 miles." The Lochsa River is suddenly on my left—a beautiful, broad, apparently deep stream.

At the Jerry Johnson campground and day-use area, I am waiting for Peter and Ron. The stream here comes around a bend, straightens, goes under a footbridge, and then bends again on its way down. The footbridge leads to a hot spring. Standing at the bridge's middle, I can see one, two, three, four, or more peaks. None of them high enough to be treeless. All of them covered in evergreen and larch. The only sound is the river, the occasional bird, the less occasional car going by. Looking down, I see the water is shallow here, the streambed is rocky. I look for fish holding behind the larger rocks, and do not see even one. Four people pass me on the footbridge. All of them say "hello" as they pass.

16

I have been wet and as cold in every part as I ever was in my life, indeed I was at one time fearfull my feet would freeze in the thin mockersons which I wore.

—William Clark, Saturday [Monday] Septr. 16th, 1805

17

NEITHER RON NOR PETER are here yet, so I put on my waders and pull the leader and fly line through my rod, then walk to the middle of the stream. And I wish I could explain the feeling. Water, hard against my calves and then knees and then thighs. Even standing still, I can feel the movement of the earth against my body. It doesn't matter if I make a single cast, or if I catch a single fish. My stomach, tonight, does not depend on my talent or my luck. Yet this is the peace for me. If I'm standing still and the water is pressing against me, or if I'm sitting still but the world is rolling under my tires, I can feel a connection to—what? Size? Enormity? Or is it just a way to confirm my hope that I will never have seen it all, that there will always be another turn in the highway or bend in the river? I cast a line toward fish I can only imagine—happily.

When Ron and Peter show up, we shake hands, happy to meet each other. Ron and I return to the water, and Peter decides to hike the banks. Neither of us catches a fish. Not even one. Not even a strike or a nibble. But the day becomes one of those days that fills the soul with what autumn can be. Each breath of cool air felt inside the lungs. Each eyeful beautiful.

We try one spot, and then we try another. We try sunny bends in the river; we try deep, shaded pools. No fish anywhere. After a while, we decide to drive downriver to see if our luck will be better elsewhere. Ron drives his car, while Peter rides in the Jeep with me. Ron knows where the good trout holes are, he says.

The valley is close enough that we cannot see Ron's car, even though we believe he's only a short distance in front of us. And we pass place after place where there should be fish. But, for a long while, we do not see Ron.

When we do see him, he's standing next to his car, which is stopped at a place called the Wilderness Restaurant. Ron's trunk is open. A little sign out front of the cafe lets us know they'll clean game for us if we wish.

Looking for a good place to fish, it seems, Ron had run over a grouse with his car, stopped, wrung its neck, and then put it in a bag in his trunk. Although he doesn't ask the restaurant staff to clean it, he shows it off to us proudly. Dinner tonight.

Just south of the Wilderness Restaurant the Selway River joins the Lochsa, and the two become the Clearwater River. This is the river once called the "Koos koos ke." The Clearwater, after some time, broadens and deepens, and I can again imagine Lewis and Clark, the speed of the canoe, the rush of water under a paddle, the hope for an ocean.

18

[T]he pleasure I now felt in having tryumphed over the rocky Mountains and decending once more to a level and fertile country where there was every rational hope of finding a comfortable subsistence for myself and party can be more readily conceived than expressed, nor was the flattering prospect of the final success of the expedition less pleasing.

—Meriwether Lewis, Sunday September 22cd, 1805

19

THERE IS A MOMENT when you know a trip has ended, even though there may be miles still to travel. It's the moment when your attention shifts—away from the present, away from a consideration of how light falls on the landscape or how beautiful and sudden a vista may be—to some point in the future. It's when you begin to think about where you're going, instead of the world that takes you there.

Driving down the valley with Peter, our conversation begins with what we're seeing. What is this place? I ask him. What kind of tree is that? But as the Clearwater Valley opens and the river gets larger, our conversation moves toward the next few days and the work we'll be doing. Our consideration of the future pauses for a minute when Peter tries to point out the house of some friends on a bluff overlooking the river—this house, he says; no, wait, that house, he thinks—but in truth our friends no longer live there. Peter is pointing out a house we once read about, a house our friends occupied in the past, while we talk about meeting these friends a few days in our future.

And soon we are talking about Nez Perce, and Coeur d'Alene, and volcanic overburdens, and paper mills, and undergraduates, and the Peace Corps, and magazines. What are the stories here? The present landscape becomes storied, and certainly rich, but also then busy with other voices. The simple surprise of it all quiets, and disappears if you're not paying attention.

The valley ends where the Clearwater joins the Snake River and a paper mill fills every possible twist of the eye. Our road turns north, and climbs toward a plateau. The sunlight is fading, and the world is turning gold and brown and a green that's nearly black. A thousand feet now higher than the riverbed, I find myself looking over my shoulder back toward the valley, and gasping.

ROAD NOTES

Sometimes the road does not give you a story. More often than not, really, what you get is a scene, a something barely caught by the corner of your eye or the depth of your hearing. You pass a red car, or you hear a voice you'd swear was a best friend from high school, or you see some funky weather, but then you're on to something else. Every tenth-of-a-mile marker, every gas station, brings another setting, another cast of characters, another bit of dialogue and intrigue. But late at night, or perhaps even years later, the fast glimpses come back. Not like nightmare, or fantasy. Just the scene itself. And perhaps a hint of something larger—something horrid, or beautiful, or just so damn crazy there ought to be a song.

Two o'clock on a Tuesday afternoon and I'm leaving Fargo in a snowstorm. Down two highway ramps, both snow covered, I'm fairly certain I'll be stuck before I even leave town. I've already spilled coffee on my lap. Snow blows into finger drifts across the gray lanes of I-29 South. It's the kind of day when normally you wouldn't begin any kind of trip. You wouldn't want to go to the grocery store, much less drive ten hours from Fargo to Kansas City.

Today the mile markers are crusted with ice and unreadable. The highway is barely visible from the powder snow that draws across it. The Jeep is in four-wheel drive. Even this early in the afternoon, the winter daylight is fading. The snow fog is so thick you can barely see the road a half mile ahead. Trucks make it even more difficult as they pass. The fences on either side of the interstate are almost completely submerged in the rising snow.

At the Abercrombie exit, excavators and bulldozers are working in the snow on the northern side of the overpass. But that's not what it looks like. It looks like they're excavating some kind of body, gashes and scars on the hillside where they're moving snow. Dark-brown, dried blood–brown earth marking where the machinery has moved.

The bulldozers and excavators are minuscule compared to the amount of snow they need to move. But I do know what they are doing. So much snow this winter. Already more than twice our normal accumulation. More in the forecast. More today. More next week. The machines are trying to create a space around the overpasses that the snow doesn't fill in so quickly. The blowing snow coming off the fields falls into the incisions. It's a good plan, unless the snow keeps coming, which it does.

As I approach the bridge, it occurs to me that there are no animals—no cows in the fields watching the cars go by, no deer, no birds on fence posts or in the air. They're all out there somewhere but hunkered down, waiting for this kind of weather to go by. And soon enough I'm back to snow cover, finger drifts, and white-knuckle driving. The landscape where it intersects the interstate seems violent, jagged. Out in the fields, of course, soft as pillows, a place to lie down and sleep forever.

6:00 A.M. AT THE Perkin's Restaurant in Alexandria, Minnesota, in the middle of October. A small adventure as I try to order just toast—to go. McDonald's isn't open yet, so that's why I am at Perkin's. We can't find toast on the register. The cashier can find just about everything else—this is her first day, and she's still being trained, she tells me—but she cannot find the button to press for toast. Rye toast. With butter.

Well, she says. At least this is more interesting than the speech she has to give for speech class later today. She's reading an essay written by a friend of hers: on suicide.

SEVEN O'CLOCK in the evening, fifty miles north of Casper, Wyoming, in late September. A curious thing happens. As the sun sets in the West, the light there moves from white, through spectacular yellows, into a kind of brown, and finally to dusk. In the East, however, a kind of response that's closer to poetry or song than anything else. The sky turns pink, and underneath that pink a layer of deep indigo blue. I've seen these colors before, but never this deep, never this rich, never this full. Cows and antelope by the scores line the highway. As I pass them at seventy-five miles an hour, I'd swear each one looks at me as if they're expecting something. As if something really big was about to happen.

⌣

ON A ROAD TRIP, sometimes all you can do is keep a list. You hold the names, wondering how each one came to be attached to the place you speed past more quickly than any animal can run. Sometimes it's the town names that seem dropped from the sky in the wrong place. Melville, North Dakota, for example. Or Voltaire, North Dakota. Sexsmith, Alberta.

For me, however, it's usually the river names. Not because they seem out of place—normally they seem much better suited to the landscape than any Rosemary Drive or West Fifty-fourth Street—but because they seem so filled with story and history. Each river name seems a promise of illumination. The San Antonio River. The Guadalupe River. The San Marcos River. Blanco River.

FOUR APACHE attack helicopters sweep low and fast over the highway sign for the LBJ Library.

A COUPLE, walking out of a highway rest stop just outside of Omaha. The woman turns to her friend and exclaims, "What would you do? I mean, really. What would you *do?*"

WALNUT CREEK. South San Gabriel River. North San Gabriel River. Lampasas River. Elm Fork of the Trinity River. Prairie Dog Town Fork of the Red River. Red River. Hickory Creek. Washita River. Little River. Cimarron River. Black Bear Creek. Red Rock Creek. Salt Fork of the Arkansas River. Chikaskia River. Ninaska River. Arkansas River. White Water River. Cottonwood River. Neosho River. Badger Creek. Frog Creek. Long Creek. Coal Creek. Rock Creek. Tequa Creek. Rock Creek. Mare de Signes River. Ottawa Creek. Wolf Creek. Bull Creek. Indian Creek. Missouri River. Todd Creek. Platte River. Bee Creek. Pigeon Creek. Dillon Creek. Hopkins Creek. Nodaway River. Kimsey Creek. Squaw Creek. Little Tarkio Creek. Tarkio River. Mill Creek. Rock Creek. Nishnabotna River. Boyer River. Soldier River. Little Sioux River. Floyd River. Big Sioux River.

FROM THE AUDIOTAPE—

Notice how when listening to the radio we always prefer the music to the DJ, always prefer the metaphor to the real life. The music brings us our memories, our hopes, our dreams in ways that are—*Whoa, shit! Now that was a pothole! Damn! Where's the coffee? Oh, great, the cup is on the floor, and most of what was in the cup is on my face. Shit. Oh, well. What was I saying? Oh, yeah.* We think the DJs are our neighbors who bring us a different kind of news.

NEAR THE NORTH Dakota border, heading home. The highway is a polished sheen of glassy ice. There are tracks occasionally on the shoulder of either side, evidence of where cars failed to keep their course. Evidence where stories began, or ended, and where memories were made, or stopped. All up and down this highway the signs that mark death spots rise from the snow. Through snow fog, what appears to be a distant farmhouse can transform suddenly into a truck fifteen feet in front of you.

As once again the light begins to dim, the ice becomes difficult to see. The median becomes filled with cars, spinning and then stuck. We all carry winter survival gear.

ELDORADO LAKE is swollen and frozen; dead trees stick out of it as small forests of barren whitewashed trunks. And I'm halfway to Dante when the radio plays "American Pie." "Do you believe in rock 'n' roll? Can music save your mortal soul? And, can you teach me how to dance real slow?"

You have to love this world.

JUST BEFORE LEAVING on a trip, I ask Yahoo Maps what the driving distance is from Fargo to San Antonio. "Driving distance was too far," it says. "Distance 1206, maximum: 1000."

VERY EARLY on a midsummer morning, well before even the beginnings of daylight, I pull into an Amoco station to top off the tank, check the oil, buy the required bag of hard candy and a cup of fresh coffee. I fill my tank and walk up to the door and find it locked. There is a sign on the front door that says, "Back in five minutes."

A young man, college age, wearing baggy pants, a sweatshirt, and tennis shoes, sits on the step outside the door. I cannot tell if he's been up all night or if, like me, he has gotten up just a short while ago, beginning this day's adventure early enough to get wherever he needs to be. In any case, he filled his car and is now waiting the five minutes.

I look at him and smile. "There may be free gas this morning," I say. He gives me a look like he hasn't thought of this yet.

I walk around back. Both garage bays are open. Tools hang within easy reach. Cases of oil and antifreeze. Radio tuned to an oldies station. The back door into the convenience store is open, and I walk in just as the missing clerk is letting the young man in from the front.

We pay for our gas, cash on the counter fast enough that we walk out together and then pause on the step.

"Have a good trip," I say.

"You too," he says. "See you later."

We smile at each other and move off into the darkness.

THE JOY OF BEGINNING

EVERY GOOD ROAD TRIP, WHETHER IT BEGINS IN SANDALS OR HIK-
ing boots, on a bicycle or in a weather-worn Jeep, whether it begins
with a train or an airplane or simply the solid closing of some door
on a summer afternoon, begins the same way. There's a look to the
sky, to check the weather. There's a press of palm to pockets, to see
if the keys are there, the compass, the money. And there's a breath,
a deep breath, to fill the lungs with the taste of this particular
morning, to test the arteries and capillaries, and to ready the body.
And then there is that step, the one that says *Let's go,* the one that
says *Move.*

This morning, in Dawson Creek, British Columbia, at the zero
mile marker for the Alaska Highway, the weather is cold and
cloudy. At the visitor and information center, cars, motor homes,
pickup trucks, and minivans crowd the parking lot. A school bus
pulls in and then blocks traffic, the driver trying to figure out where
to squeeze. License plates from Pennsylvania, Alaska, British Columbia, Minnesota, Texas, Alberta, Saskatchewan, Kentucky.

Tourists with cameras slung over their necks wander from sign
to sign, reading about the history of Dawson Creek or the Alcan

Highway. They wander in and out of the Dawson Creek Art Gallery and Museum, a massive reconditioned grain elevator, then the travelers' center, a restored train station, or an old rail car—the Blue Goose Caboose—which sells ice cream and Coca Cola. Inside the travelers' center, they paw over T-shirts and caps. They hold up postcards, each showing some sepia-tinted vision of the road in construction or mayhem, then ask the clerk for news. If she tells them the road is fine, no major washouts, no chassis-bending holes in the construction sites, no bears lifting compact cars like lunch pails, you can see in their faces that they simply don't want to believe her.

A few steps to the right, behind the racks for souvenirs, a doorway opens into the pioneer heritage museum. A stuffed black bear and grizzly bear, a stuffed mountain goat and timber wolf, bald eagle, golden eagle, falcons. Artifacts of living in the old days here—combs and tables and outfits, dresses and work clothes. Plate glass to protect the fabric and wood and metal. Yet, the people remain in the first room. One lonely man in a bandanna watches a video about the construction of the Alcan Highway.

This is one of the starting lines, jumping-off points, leaving places. As far as the myth will tell us, this parking lot, with the white mile marker at the far end, is the border between what we know—the grocery stores and hardware stores, the little leagues and church meetings, the routines of work and family—and the extraordinary. This place is the beginning of the Alaska Highway, the last road in North America that people still dream about, that last road that people come to drive—not to get to the end of it, not simply to say, "I've been to Alaska" or "I've been in the Yukon." They come here, just as I've come here, for the road itself, for the story, for the apparent if not evident risk, for the chance to see something new, and to have that chance with every turn of a tire.

A family poses under the Alcan Highway sign for a picture, all smiles and bravado. In the parking lot, new license plates for Washington, Michigan, Virginia.

❂

As I ROLL out of Dawson Creek, past the Ford dealer, past the Ramada Limited, past the espresso shop, it is possible to wonder what romance there still is to this road, and if there is anything real about it. A packaged adventure is no adventure at all. A few thousand miles of photo opportunities, tourist cafes, planned and groomed hiking trails are not at all what the stories promise.

And there are stories already. There is the early one, remembered for its theme yet otherwise lost to the confusion of youth, which simply told me this road was here. This road, built so fast that bulldozers routinely passed the surveyors, built through the hardest part of the wilderness, built in a land with the coldest water, the angriest bears, the hungriest wolves, the most spectacular fish, the most lethal weather, was for me the same thing as Everest or Antarctica. You hear a story and you can feel it inside you, a calling, a small shift in the way the blood flows through your brain and then into your legs. You hear this story and you know what really matters is that there still are places where the world can open. And before you die, this is what you must see.

Other stories follow, and each one of them adds to the desire. There is the story told to me by friends, for example, who were driving north out of Fort Nelson on the way to Yellowknife. There was the flat tire, then the rocks in the windshield, the normal details of a road trip going well, and there was the added spice of a cafe they visited, an improbable one filled with flies and offering microwaved pizza. But what struck me was the showdown they had with a bison. Turning a corner, they found it standing in the middle of the narrow gravel road, facing them. Their car, a Taurus, slowed and then stopped. Bull and bison faced each other, each one breathing out smoke, each one filled with an idea. In the car, someone asked, "Do you think we should lock the doors?"

The road story in North America is the story of the unexpected, and the following grace. There are, of course, the stories of bandits or blizzards, black ice and multiple deaths. But more often than not what we remember, and what feeds us, is the mundane suddenly opening toward intimacy and welcome. Driving up here yesterday, there are two stories I'll save.

A mile or so before the Cottonwood Esso station, a sign proclaimed a steak sandwich. I was hungry, so I pulled in. The left side of the building was the station, the convenience store, a clerk accepting money for gasoline. The right side was the restaurant. When I entered, an elderly woman with gray hair, glasses, and a cigarette sat at one of the Formica tables. She nodded at me. Nobody was working behind the counter.

"Busy place," I said.

She said, "Well, it was about five minutes ago."

I waited a few minutes. Then I asked her, "Is anybody home?" She nodded toward the door to the kitchen. I walked back and looked in—not a soul. I looked at her. "Well, nobody's here now." Her eyebrows went up in surprise. I started to walk to the door, thinking the steak sandwich would simply be a sign and not a reality, when a man did appear from the back.

Very friendly, very outgoing, he said, "What can I get for you?"

"I saw the sign for the steak sandwich."

He laughed. "We can do that."

I said, "Is this a steak sandwich as in a piece of steak on a piece of bread on a plate, or is this something I can eat in the car?"

He said, "No, this is on a plate and sit down."

I said, "Nah, I've got to keep going."

He said, "But I can put it between two pieces of garlic bread for you!"

I said, "That sounds marvelous."

He disappeared into the kitchen, reappeared a minute later to ask me if I wanted any veggies. "A few onions," I told him. He disappeared again. When he appeared a few minutes later, he had no less than a one inch–thick steak between two fat pieces of garlic bread, sautéed onions on top, a little box to put it in. It *was* marvelous. I told him that I'd stop back by on the way back south if the sandwich was good. The lady at the table smiled and nodded.

I cannot tell you if he wanted to make that sandwich for the money, which wasn't very much, or for the simple pleasure of company in an otherwise lonely Esso station. But he smiled at me, asked about the drive, and the sandwich was very good.

And then this one, too. Yesterday, at the Beaver Lodge Husky station, I pulled in to get some gas. As I walked in, a man was talking and laughing with the clerk. The clerk looked at me and said, "Old jobs we're talking about."

I said, "I've had a few of those."

He waved me over like we knew each other, like we'd gone to school together, like we were friends. He said, "Well, I used to work at this restaurant that just closed down in town. I was a waiter, a busboy, a dishwasher, a prep cook, and cook all on the same shift. Not many people can do that."

I said, "Nope, not many can."

He said, "A while back, it was my day off. I went off and had a few drinks with some friends. The boss called me up and asked me if I could come in. I said, 'No, I really can't. I've had a few drinks. This would not be a good thing.' And so she fired me."

He said, "Now, I told all the waitresses at this place where I had the few drinks the story. Not one of them went back to that restaurant ever again. They all loved me."

I smiled at the guy and said, "Some things do turn out for the better, I suppose."

He smiled. "Have a good one," he said.

"I will."

Small stories, both of them. Neither of them happened on the Alaska Highway, and they could have happened anywhere. But ordinary kindness is oftentimes invisible at home. On the road, the blessing is that you are the stranger, the foreign one, the one who looks for clues in everything because you do not yet know what matters. On the road, every welcome is joy.

Yesterday, the fifteen-hour drive from Regina to Dawson Creek began with prairie, with sunshine on golden fields of canola and wheat, and turned a little darker with every kilometer west. North and west of Edmonton, the land became forest, commercial forest, straight-line rows of trees for the lumber industry. Large stands of birch and fir. Occasionally I would come to the top of a ridge and there would be farmland, cattle ranches, buffalo ranches, but then the road would drop or make a turn and, once again, I'd be back in the forest, passing lumber truck after lumber truck.

Forestry. And oil. Lots of forestry. Lots of oil. Pipelines coming up to the roadside. Route 43 is called Moose Road, and there are large signs saying, "Watch Out for the Moose." Not a single one appeared, though I looked very hard. Fifteen hundred miles from home in a town called Valleyview, I turned off Route 43 and onto Route 34, and I got the first glimpse of the Rocky Mountains off in the far western distance.

SOME DAYS BEGIN like symphonies. Some days begin like jazz. And some days begin like a third grader learning to play the drums. I'm not very far out of Fort St. John, only seventy-three kilometers away from Dawson Creek, and I just got pulled over by the RCMP! A police car pulled up behind me, siren off but lights flashing. I got out of the Jeep as an officer got out of the patrol car, and I handed him my license before he could ask for it.

"What did I do wrong?" I asked.

"What did I do wrong?" he repeated.

He asked for my registration, and I showed him that as well.

"Your tires," he said. "We got a call from a man back in town. Black Jeep, foreign plates, oversized tires that aren't covered."

I looked at him, then at my tires, amazed. My tires, a little larger than stock, are hardly monsters. I explained to him that, well, in the States, these are considered covered. He sat in his car for a while and talked with his partner and then on the radio while I paced around the Jeep. Gravel roads and busted windshields, I thought. Nonsense, I thought! If he writes me a ticket, or makes me buy mud flaps, I'll surely say something I'll regret. But when he came back, handed me my license and registration, he couldn't have been more pleasant. No ticket. Not even a warning, or a suggestion. He asked me what I'm doing up here, and I told him I'm working on a book.

"Think this will be in it?" he asked, smiling.

"Almost certainly," I said.

He began to walk back to the patrol car, then stopped and turned back to me.

"The guy who called," he said. "He calls a lot."

In the Jeep and up to speed, passing through a town called Charlie Lake, I found myself watching the rearview mirror more closely than the road ahead.

Odd starts can find their own rhythm, and the bad drumming of a beginner can turn, with luck, into a feel for syncopation and cadence. Past Fort St. John and Charlie Lake, the Alaska Highway stretches out and begins to find itself. Even though the road is smooth and even and well paved, tremendous forests line both sides and you can feel the distance inside them. On the advice of a hotel clerk in Dawson Creek, I stop to fish at the Sikanni Chief River, only to find the water too high and muddy for decent tries.

Farther on, I stop at Bucking Horse Provincial Park, where the Bucking Horse River is soft and clear. I lose a dry fly, watch it float downstream through swirls and eddies, and nothing rises to taste either it or its replacement. From there on out, I drive to make some time, so it seems perfectly natural that I should discover a llama has gotten loose and is wandering the center of the Alaska Highway. A dark-brown llama. It has a rope around its neck, frayed and broken a few feet from the knot. It must have jumped the fence. Two other llamas look longingly over the fence at the one that's gotten away. The liberated llama just looks confused.

Pulling around, then back up through the gears—I want to go fast, though I'm not sure why—I find myself wondering about the immensity of the stories I do not know, the clues I am missing. There is tremendous wilderness here, and tremendous industry too. I've already passed a small plant for Canadian Natural Resources, Ltd. A pipeline for natural gas, I suppose, with a small fire-topped tower for venting. I've passed a compressor station for West Coast Energy. Earlier in the day, there was the Canadian crude-separators site. Oil and natural gas and timber, all of these things are sitting right here. Signs along the forest say, "Reforested 1978, Reforested 1989," almost like PR to make you believe the forests are coming back after the logging industry has come through. Occasionally, there are service roads leading from the highway off to the south. Large signs in front of an entrance say, "Do Not Enter. Poisonous Gas Area." A little farther on, another sign says, "Do Not Enter. Poisonous H_2S gas." On the highway, the signs say, "Warning: Caribou on Highway."

When I get to the accident, I am surprised by how normal it seems. Not to me, of course, but to the many people standing around. A woman and two small children, one looking to be two or three years old, the other less than a year, are standing beside the road. Their car, a bright-red Chevrolet, is nose deep in the drainage. The kids look exhausted. The woman looks calm, or dazed, or in shock. A group of men and another woman is standing around her, now at the back of a red pickup truck, talking. No one is rushing. No one is applying bandages or offering confessions. I slow and then stop to see if I can help, and it turns out the woman with the children had fallen asleep at the wheel. She had gone off the road on one side, pulled back, overcorrected, and gone off the road on the other side and wound up in a ditch. The people in the other car, three men and a nurse from an oil rig crew, watched the whole thing happen.

Everyone is all right, but the Chevy isn't running. Its fan belt, a serpentine used to run the whole of the motor, has disappeared. So while we don't need an ambulance, we do need to get these people toward home.

The woman and her kids get in the pickup truck. The nurse drives. Two of the oilmen climb up to ride in the truck's bed. The remaining man, who tells me his name is Red, climbs in the Jeep with me. We're an hour outside of Fort Nelson.

What can you learn in an hour with a stranger? The normal questions go by quickly. Why are you here? Where have you been? What do you think so far? Red learns I'm just another tourist, driving around, looking at mountains and valleys. What I learn, though, is that Red is in love.

"I'll never leave B.C.," he tells me. "I mean, I'll go on vacation and stuff, but I'll never move away. I just love the bush too much."

Red's job is to walk the pipeline, inspecting it, looking for problems. He wants to retire by the time he's forty or forty-five—not with a pension, but with savings. "They pay us pretty well," he says. Then he wants to open a small store of his own.

"Ever run into bears on the pipeline?" I ask.

"No," he says. "The worst thing that ever happened to me was I got beaver fever after crossing this one small stream. Took me a while to get over it."

The camps and towns around here are tough places, he tells me. Oil rig towns. Hard places, yet also places where the people will give you the shirt off their back. He tells me one story about a family whose engine threw a rod and they didn't have any money with them, at least not enough for a new or rebuilt engine. The town got together, rebuilt the engine for them, and sent them on their way. The family sent money back, which the town returned, saying, you know, good neighbors are good neighbors.

"That's impressive," I say.

"I'll never leave B.C.," he says.

We ride in silence for a while, watching the forests and hills go by, then Red starts to chuckle. "I forgot to tell you," he says. "You didn't see it, but a while back on the other side of the trees there was a small airstrip. Guy back there is a bush pilot, one of the best. He's got this tiny little plane, and he used to fly up behind people he knew on the road and put one of his wheels on the cab of the truck. You'd never hear him or see him until he was right on top of you, and then you'd have an airplane on your truck."

Red's smile is both proud and incredulous.

"Let me guess," I say. "You'll never leave B.C."

At the Fort Nelson Husky station, the woman and her kids settle into a cafe for whatever comes next. The oil crew and nurse reassemble in the truck, Red and I shake hands, and they are off.

❧

JUST WEST of Fort Nelson, a large bison herd grazes in a field. Another sign warns me to watch out for caribou on the highway. For the first time, the Alaska Highway heads into the heart of the mountains. Peaks appear as if suddenly on both sides of the roadway, sharp and dramatic against blue sky and bright sun. It's midsummer, but there is still snow in the gullies here and in the shadowed bends of rivers and runoff. Forests of aspen, white spruce. Each bend in the road brings a new vista, thrilling because I'm close to a wall, craning my head and neck to see its top, amazed at the simple size and weight of so much rock—or thrilling because suddenly there is no rock at all and I can see miles up a valley toward some other pass, wishing myself there just a little bit faster.

I'm approaching Stone Mountain, Summit Lake, and then Summit Pass, the highest point on the route. I'm looking at the scale of the earth, the cliffs and valleys and walls and peaks, nearly ecstatic with such theater, but when I slow for a corner the drama moves much closer. A black bear grazes in the brush at the end of the highway clearing, just outside the trees. It moves steadily, sniffing one way and then another, and does not look at me even though I've matched its pace. When it moves back into the trees I step on the gas to get up the hill, and then almost immediately press the brake pedal hard. Stone sheep, six or eight of them, stand in the middle of the road. Brown-gray, adults with horns, offspring a bit skittish, they browse the road's edge. As I move closer, they step indifferently to one side.

Another turn in the road and I'm at Stone Mountain and Summit Lake. Summit Pass, still a bit ahead, is only 4,250 feet above sea level, so this place cannot be above the tree line, but nonetheless there are no trees. Stone Mountain. Summit Lake, narrow between two peaks, bright blue and calm, reflects the evening light and the gray light of the peaks. A pullout and campground border the lake on the eastern side, and when I pull in all the spots are taken. To stretch my legs a bit, I stop at a small boat launch and unpack my fly rod.

Two casts, and a man walks up.

"Any luck?" he asks. His voice is thick with Louisiana or Georgia.

"Not yet."

"Do you really think I need to buy a license?"

"Yes."

He walks away. Two casts later, maybe three, an Asian man is beside me. He watches one cast.

"Are there fish in this lake?"

❂

BACK ON THE ROAD and I'm a little bit worried. I still have a long way to go to make a hotel where they are expecting me, and the day is ending. On the east side of Summit Lake, I pass caribou and then moose. More stone sheep. Another black bear.

The road is turning bad. Broken pavement and gravel, gravel that kicks up thick blond clouds of dust that hold in the air, and potholes big enough to swallow a dream. Very slow going, thirty miles an hour at best, and yet nearly magical because the twilight lingers and it never gets dark. There's a full moon behind me, and a steady dusk in front. The Jeep has shadows on both sides.

♣

AT THE TOAD RIVER Café and Lodge, another single-story log cabin–style building on the side of the road, I stop to fill up with gas, walk into the cafe, and watch large meals of pork chops and steak, potatoes, and salad being served to a full house by a lone college-age waitress. Two men in their fifties each order single rooms in the lodge.

It's dinnertime, or after. Certainly stopping time, too. But not for me.

What I do not know until I walk in here, though, is that this place is famous. The ceilings of the dining room, the hallways, the area by the register are all covered with caps. According to the waitress, who also works the register, 5,295 caps to be exact. A few boxloads more in the basement waiting to be put up.

"You going to donate yours?" she asks.

I scan the ceilings. Caps from Wonder Bread. Caps from, and signed by, the crew of the *Oprah Winfrey Show*. It's an interesting way to spend some time, looking at who's passed by on this road and who's felt the small need to leave their mark.

Another man asks, "Do you guys sell beer?"

The lady says, "No, we don't."

He says, "Where's the closest place?"

She says, "Well, you could go to Fort Nelson. That's about six or seven hours behind us, or you could go to Watson Lake. That's about three hours in front. You might be able to get to the lodge at Muncho Lake in time and sit in their restaurant, but they don't do off-sales."

Everybody chuckles.

While a man makes a phone call in the cafe, his wife paces around in the restaurant. The lady at the desk says, "Can I get you anything?"

She says, "No, I've got to stand up. I've been sitting for far too long." She has a smile on her face, a weary one, though also satisfied.

This is, after all, a stop on the Alaska Highway. The men and women at the tables in the Toad River Café have spent this last day among bears and sheep and caribou, cliffs and valleys and rivers and lakes. This is *the trip*. They might have 5,295 hats hanging from the ceiling at the Toad River Café, and a very pleasant waitress, but nothing compares to the anticipation of the next curve where the world is remade.

I do not know a soul in this room tonight. I cannot tell you anything about their lives, their families, their jobs or careers, their worries, or their accomplishments. Honestly, in this place, I'm not sure any of it matters. What we share is the simple truth that twilight in the Canadian Rockies is a beautiful thing. The mountains facing east turn dark, first green and then a gray and then heading toward blackness. The mountains facing west are illuminated with the particular glow of sunset light. There is a sadness, a nostalgia perhaps, in the earth growing darker. But at the very same moment there is also a shock, a surprised, pleased, opening, and exciting thing in the lungs when some light catches someplace and the hills come alive with the sparkle you haven't seen all day.

Despite the rest for food and the stillness of sleep, what we are in this place is in motion. And what I'm thinking, as I'm pulling away once more and heading north and west, is that this act of travel, this motion, is when we are happiest. I honestly believe that the human being is happiest in motion, or, better yet, in anticipation. Anticipation is probably our sweetest state. The first trip, the border of a land or our own experience, the frontier, the ongoing and unrealized quest, the thing we are planning, the places on any map we have yet to fill in—these are the things that bind us with our own history, with our understanding of what it means to be human. Anticipation is always exciting. Even when it's dangerous, it's a thrill. When we are in motion, each bend in the road, each new face of a mountain, tells us that the world is indeed precious, and our experience opens. There are larger and bigger and more things out there. We are unable to imagine the fullness of what lies around any corner, and so we head to that corner earnestly, and as fast as we can.

❧

THE DAY GROWS darker, but Muncho Lake appears to have its own light. Deep blue and green (a guidebook tells me because of copper oxide leaching into the lake), it's another long and narrow water between ranges of mountains. Bulldozers work at clearing rocks from the roadway where a flash flood or cloudburst had carried them. I pass the Rocky Mountain Lodge, then stop, turn around, and head back. The lodge is a chalet, and I'm thinking of places to stay on the way back.

The lodge is beautiful. The night clerk, a young woman who tells me she's a year-rounder, now in her third year, gives me the brochures, and what I read is that this building is the largest log structure in British Columbia. The fireplace is forty-five feet high. The owners emigrated from Switzerland, and the place has the feel of the Alps. A floatplane flies guests to remote lakes and streams each morning. The food is overwhelming.

Standing there, I notice in her brochures that the Liard River Hot Springs are just forty minutes away. I hadn't realized they were so close, or that it was so late I might be passing them in darkness.

"I saw a story about that place on TV back home," I tell her. "A grizzly bear mauled a tourist in one of the pools. It pretty much ate up one leg before it was shot and killed by another tourist. The guy who was attacked seemed to have recovered, and the guy who did the shooting was given a fine for illegally having a gun in the park."

She smiles at me and says, "That was a big story. Actually, the springs were closed for two weeks this spring because there was another grizzly bear in the area. It was moved." She says, "But that's not one of the things we normally tell the tourists—or the guests."

There are always stories. Evident stories and invisible ones, too. The bear that mauled one tourist and was shot by another made television back in Minnesota. I sat up late one night learning that the attacking bear had zero body fat and was, in fact, starving. This worried the biologists because it meant something was going on in the forest that they didn't understand.

Back in the Jeep, racing to get to the springs before they close, I slow before crossing the Liard River because three horses wander the roadway. On the other side of the bridge, a blond yearling wolf trots in the roadside brush. When I stop to take a picture, it stops and looks at me straight on, then moves away. Just beyond it, three very large bison graze the same brush.

I make it to the hot springs park before the gates are closed, and begin to run down the boardwalk to the pools, then realize there are a good many people here, and no one else is in a hurry. I look in my guidebook and learn that this boardwalk traverses a wetland that supports more than 250 boreal forest plants. There are fourteen species of orchid, and a host of plants that survives this far north only because of the springs. I slow my walk considerably.

At the first set of pools, children play downstream to the left, where the water is slightly warmer than a normal bath. Adults sit on submerged benches without moving much in a center pool, where the water is a good bit warmer, and no one has the courage for the pool most upstream before the rocks, where the water seems nearly to boil.

Without bathing suit, all I can do is take off my boots and socks, roll up my jeans a bit, and sit on the steps. It all looks very lush, I think. The thickness of the trees, the plants, the steam from the water and the earth. The two men sharing a bench in the middle pool quietly compare their travel routes. Highway numbers, turns right or left, road conditions, what they've seen. It's all impressive, but as understated as a pilot describing the weather over the Grand Canyon or the Himalayas. What I find most interesting, though, is the fact that neither of them asks where the other is going. Neither one of them ever mentions a destination. The road is their conversation. The road, and its promise, is what brought them to this pool. The kids in the next pool are loud in their glee. In the rich twilight, the adults grow quiet.

❖

So THEN IT IS midnight, and after. Alone on the Alaska Highway, heading toward Watson Lake, still 150 miles to go, and then tomorrow on toward Whitehorse. The day after that, I hope to leave the Alaska for the Yukon Highway and the road toward Dawson City. Then the Dempster Highway and Inuvik in the Northwest Territories. I'd lingered too long, too mesmerized by the simple heat of a thermal pool, the comfort it offered my feet and legs. At first I was going to spend only fifteen minutes, perhaps half an hour. But that short time went quickly, and I was not ready to leave.

One A.M. Perhaps two. And as I come around a bend in an otherwise deserted stretch of road, suddenly both sides of the road are on fire. Flames, twenty or thirty feet high. Behind them, and in them, I can see what look like glowing animal eyes moving slowly, deliberately, toward me.

My headlights catch the reflective orange vest of a highway signalman. I slow, and pull up next to him. He grins at me. I grin at him. I am still half expecting a three-headed dog.

Neither of us says anything for a while. Both of us simply watch the fire and the work.

"Is this normal?" I ask, finally, not knowing really what else to say.

"For here it is," he says.

He goes on to explain that this is simply how they keep the highway shoulders clear. We are too far away to haul the brush anywhere, so in the middle of the night, when there is little traffic, bulldozers and Bobcats (their headlamps are what I imagined to be animal eyes) push the brush into piles, and the crews set them aflame. A large water truck sits beside the road in case the fires grow out of hand.

After a minute, he lets me continue. But all the way to Watson Lake, and even after, that question and his answer stay with me.

"Is this normal?"

"For here it is."

I cannot imagine a better question, or a better answer, to explain why I am here. To explain why any of us travel. To explain our hopes as well as our desperation.

❦

SHOW ME A PLACE where no one has been, and I will go there. No matter how hard, or how expensive, the blank spaces on the map have already claimed me, have always claimed me. And I am neither alone, nor unusual. But is it possible for there to be any such place? Marco Polo went exploring and found an Asia filled with art and armies, peddlers and poets. John Smith walked ashore and met Pocahontas. In 1960, Jacques Piccard and Don Walsh took a look out the view port of the bathyscaphe *Trieste* to see the silt at the bottom of the Challenger Deep in the Mariana Trench, 36,198 feet below the surface of the Pacific Ocean, the deepest spot in the world, to find fish waving fins back at them. There are footprints and tire tracks on the moon, and robots on Mars. Every few months, our telescopes see just a little bit farther around the bend in the universe.

Every few minutes, another soul begins a trip on the Alaska Highway, or any other road whose shape and color and feel are mysteries. Every few minutes, someone feels the dirt under their boots or the gravel under their tires, and the world becomes an opening place. It doesn't matter how many have come before us. It matters completely that we join the history.

This evening, now very late, finally at an inn and listening to the ticking of the Jeep's engine cooling as I remove my bag, I am not settling into any kind of reverie about the past day's stories. Tomorrow I will drive from Watson Lake to Whitehorse. The day after that, Whitehorse to Dawson City. And after that, one lonely road to cross the Arctic Circle. What fills my heart is the fact that I have no idea at all what the earth will offer tomorrow, or the days after. Today has been a very good day. And there is always the promise that tomorrow will be larger than my capacity to imagine it.

Is this normal?

For here it is.

POINTED HOME – 1991

Day One

WHEN YOU BEGIN A ROAD TRIP, THERE ARE THINGS YOU BELIEVE. It's not a matter of choice. You believe, for example, that your destination will be there. You believe that the town or the city or the lake or the campsite will be where you last left it, or where you've been promised it waits. You do not wonder about asteroids, rapture, or the sudden strike of a nuclear war in an otherwise peaceful time. When you first turn the key and feel an engine's spark, when you put the car in a gear to begin, it would be too much to say you're even worried about these things. Worry implies a perceived risk. *Faith* would be a better word. When you begin a road trip, you have faith that the world this day will be the one you know.

SUNDAY, 3:46 P.M.
This particular Sunday afternoon in Washington, D.C., the weather is hot. I can feel my shirt beginning to stick to my skin. There aren't any clouds, but a humid haze makes seeing anything at real distances difficult. The buses and taxis and automobiles at National

Airport churn around the circular drive, bringing their passengers to whatever ticket counter they want, whatever destination their money can afford. The colors of metal and luggage and clothing and skin are muted in the air.

The day is visually close, the visual spectrum of light overfilled by so many expressions of to-come and to-go. And there's an aural element, too. In short-term parking lot A, just outside the terminal for Northwest Airlines, I can hear the cars and buses and taxis in their manic creep toward and away from their stops. I can hear the airplanes on the other side of the terminal building as they taxi and rush and rocket and brake. But it all comes to me muffled, as if the air were overloaded by so many engines, too filled to carry sound correctly.

I am about to drive across the country. My wife, Maureen, and my daughter, Kate, have just taken off on a flight for Minneapolis, then another flight to Fargo, then a short drive across the Red River of the North to our home in Moorhead, Minnesota. I am not with them. In my imagination at least, Kate is being lulled to sleep now by the muffled sound of jet engines, and Maureen is being handed a cup of tea by a flight attendant who tells her she looks like her child, while I am still waiting to back out of my parking space.

Just a few months ago, the call had come from my parents. It was time for a family reunion. Almost everyone had the same part of their calendars open, so arrangements were made. Maureen and I even decided we would make a vacation out of it, take a bit more time for ourselves. We decided we would drive out of Moorhead, visit Chicago, the lake front, the old high school, the homes and streets and neighborhoods that contained and directed my world, the sights of my growing up, then arrive in Free Union, Virginia, outside Charlottesville, just before the rest of the relations. We decided we would take our time, live our own schedules. And we decided Maureen and Kate would fly back. There was little sense in putting our one-year-old daughter through a forced march–type drive west (the scenic trip east was OK—we could stop when and wherever).

So here I am. The cars behind me have a strategic advantage; I've pulled maybe halfway out of my spot, but they've got position. I've got half the country to travel, and I can't get out of short-term parking.

I'm not going to travel this country as most writers would want to travel it, stopping in at this hamlet or that burg, visiting with Grandma this, Grandpa that, uncovering the idiosyncratic quirks of making lives count. Instead, I am going to travel the way most Americans do, as quickly as possible—the interstate highways, drive-through food, a brief stop at a hotel, and then on the road again, speeding most of the time—to see if I can't articulate, in one way or another, what it is to travel long distances by ground these days. To see what, if anything, can be learned or felt so close to trees and farm animals and the water of rivers all going by at more than a mile a minute. To listen to the echoes of my brain and hear how they have changed.

I really can't wait. I like to drive. I like the shifting perspectives and the sudden vistas. I like rising from flatlands into mountains, then down again toward rivers and fog at night. And I am happy, overjoyed really, to be alone. Whatever I learn or feel will be my own.

3:51 P.M.

I finally put my car in forward. A middle-aged man driving a Honda is either kind or believes I am tired enough of waiting to think about a dent in his car. There's a long line of cars standing back from the toll booth, and this is an expensive lot. Of course, now that I'm in a forward gear, the line of cars has stopped.

4:06 P.M.

I'm joining Interstate 66, heading west. My car comes up slowly to speed, settles in between the cars and trucks. Other drivers here know their way around. I find myself rubbernecking to see if that road sign wasn't the one I needed, then cursing when a truck cuts me off.

As I entered the highway an America West jet came in low for a landing at National Airport. Low enough I could imagine touching it. I've passed the Pentagon, the Iwo Jima Memorial. Off to my right now is Memorial Bridge, and I discover it's difficult, with Maureen and Kate flying, not to think of the Air Florida flight some winters ago that didn't make it very far past National Airport. Not to remember the helicopter and the man who kept passing the lifeline to those others he would save before he lost his own life.

Essays and articles and even a movie have turned this man's death into a heroic act. His self-sacrifice an example of the inherent nobility of the human spirit. But all that is really analysis and conjecture, a type of flashlight shining into a cave or darkened room. The fact of the matter is a plane went up and then right back down. The fact of the matter is people died suddenly and out of context.

And the fact of the matter is we are more afraid of this type of death than perhaps any other. We admire the man who passed the lifeline over to others because he was able, in the frozen Potomac River, to create a context for his death, to summon up a meaning in his leaving. We are more afraid, I think, of becoming out of context than anything else. Being eaten by a shark is less tragic than dying alone, forgotten or in a crowd. We define ourselves by context—our jobs and homes and clothes and relatives—and we build that context toward the day we look back over it and take our leave. That context is how we identify ourselves. But to lose that context, to become part of some other definition, could defeat the work of a life. The individual who becomes only part of a number, the good father or mother who becomes part of the faceless dead at a plane crash, is a tremendous loss. Were Maureen and Katherine to fall out of the sky today, I fear that crash would be their definition—the largest connection I could offer from their lives to any listener.

As I merge with traffic these thoughts are enhanced and more troubled when I notice Florida cars have a license plate design I haven't seen before—the *Challenger* space shuttle.

4:19 P.M.

"Prepare for Sudden Aggravation—Beltway Widening."

4:25 P.M.

I'm in something called the I-270 Technology Corridor, the fact revealed by a sign with a yellow ribbon and an American flag. As I'm joining the express lanes of I-270 North, I'm passed by a Mercedes like I'm driving backward. The Mercedes's license plate reads "Diplomat."

This car goes by me, I look at the other cars, the road around us all, and I am struck by the fact that I-66 and I-495 and I-270, despite their designations, are not really interstate highways. They just don't fit the image. Sure, they span the borders of states and the district, but they have neither the breadth nor the breath. They don't have the vistas. With all the office buildings, the mass-quaint duplex complexes, the malls coming up to the interstate shoulder, these roads have nothing of the romance to them. They do not imply the type of freedom we want to attach to open and endless highways. They're not a part of the stereotype. These are commuter shoots, short hops. The license plates around me are all Virginia or Maryland or D.C. Quite a few read "Diplomat." And while this is, perhaps, the world's most cosmopolitan city in terms of who comes and who goes, the people who travel these roads tend to come and go locally only.

These are staff roads, roads from home to office, from office to office, from consulate to airport, from here to here. There are Fords and Chevys, Oldsmobiles and Pontiacs, Hondas and Toyotas, and it is not uncommon to see the odd Ferrari, another diplomat racing by in his Turbo Saab. But the community here is not the community of the interstate highway. What binds people here is not a sense of great distance, a sense of great time, a shared sense of experiencing a common day of road and weather. Instead, this is the community of a city, a particular and consuming routine, and those who must come and go from it each day.

Developing community, I think, is the only real topic for the human endeavor. Placement within or displacement from a community, definitions of likes and dislikes forming their own communities. Our religion and science and arts and humanities are all dedicated toward defining, illustrating, arguing, and extending the borders of community. In Washington and Baltimore now the radio stations give evidence of a hundred communities. Two cities, a hundred neighborhoods, grocery store chains, sports teams, rock fans, classical music fans, jazz fans, country fans, news and pop fans. Out here on the highway, each of us alone in our car is as isolated, perhaps, as human beings can really be from a sense of place—but not perhaps from a sense of belonging. I am a member of a listening audience. I share something with others who listen to the same radio waves, now carrying Stanley Turrentine.

Traveling more than sixty miles an hour, more than a mile a minute, to or from something, through the whiz-bang imagination of a "technology corridor," however, the sense of community becomes diffused and problematic. I'm closer to the several thousand people I will never meet who are listening to the same jazz radio station I am—closer in terms of emotion, of sentiment, of life philosophy and moral vision, perhaps—than I am to the people traveling this road with me, than I am to the man in the car next to me. He's a good-looking guy in a white dress shirt, loose tie, light-brown hair. He's somewhere in his thirties. His fingers play the steering wheel; I assume he's listening to music. Physically, we're only about seven feet apart. He could be listening to the same radio station I am. He could have in front of him a transcontinental drive, as I do. He could have been born in Kansas City, raised outside Chicago, spent some years in New England and Dixie, as I have. Hell, we could know each other. We could be close. Yet he could be ready to pull off at the next exit, heading toward a home and context I can't possibly imagine. We could be irreparably far apart. And that's the thing about the real interstates. When other communities fail, they provide a context of their own.

4:42 P.M.

I-270 North is where I first believe I am on an interstate highway. I'm beginning to lose Washington's jazz station, and I've come across the first farm visible from the roadway, a dozen Hereford cattle grazing on a hillside turned brown from heat. It feels good for this grandson of a Danish dairy farmer to be passing cattle, having just been passed by a car with an Ohio plate, being followed by a car with Maryland plates, my own plates from Minnesota, coming up on towns named Barnesville and Hyattstown, America the beautiful. I relax a bit, find a clearer station on the radio, look at hills more than traffic.

4:49 P.M.

I notice the cars in the other lanes, the oncoming traffic, suddenly have their lights on. The sky in front of me to the north and west is a deepening gray-black and blue, and I can see the echoes of lightning roll out of the clouds. I reach and turn my own lights on, and I wait for the rain. When I join I-70 West and am met by rain and lightning, in the near distance through the haze I can make out the beginnings of mountains—the foothills of the Appalachians—even though the sky swells as I cross Beaver Creek outside Smithsburg and Boonsboro.

The rainstorm ends as quickly as it begins, though the sky retains its dark loom, and when I take the time to look away from the sky toward the surrounding earth, I see I-70 West has become a true interstate. Two lanes west, two lanes east, road signs for the Ramadas, the Sheratons, the Super 8s, the Holiday Inns and McDonald's and Burger Kings. The license plates here are becoming more diverse. The countryside has become completely farmland. In the distance there are mountains, sharp and gentle hills, silos and barns and animals and corn that, if not this week, will come into harvest soon.

5:18 P.M.

The sky hasn't exactly cleared, although it's brightened considerably. A line of antique cars is heading east on the other side of the freeway. The air has become steamy after the rain, and the temperature has dropped fifteen degrees. The cool breeze from the open windows feels good as it rushes over my neck and stirs the air in the car.

A foreign car with fins and aeroskirts speeds by me at twice my sixty miles an hour. The exit to Interstate 81 comes and goes.

5:44 P.M.

"Welcome to Pennsylvania. America Starts Here."

The sky is turning gray again with the sunshine behind me. Mist and rain in front. National Public Radio has been bringing me the news from Houston, from Los Angeles, from New York City with a bond-traders scandal, the hourly doings of President George Bush. So I can't help but wonder—if the sign is true, if America starts here at the border of Pennsylvania—what is it I'm leaving behind?

Most of us who live in the Midwest would enjoy the idea that New York and Boston and Washington are not really part of America, not really a part of the national character or image or way of thinking, more foreign than the tenth planet. But at the same time we accept what those cities send our way. We accept their fashion as most current, their money as most important, their decisions as the ones we follow. New York opera is definitive. Washington politics are the most properly despised. Boston's version of the revolution is the one for our textbooks.

I would argue in favor of this sign. No one looks for the "real" America in Manhattan. When pollsters want to take the temperature of "real" or "normal" Americans, we find them in Iowa and Kansas. Welcome to the "Real" United States of America, I think. Please forgive us the colonies—they're getting old.

An entire group of cars—fifteen, maybe twenty, of us—goes by a speed trap, the officers sitting slightly off the highway just behind a clump of bushes. The officers don't come out, and every single one us is just-so-slightly speeding.

Just inside Pennsylvania the mostly smooth pavement turns to grooved pavement and the mountains once again come close to the highway. We turn left, we turn right—sweeping curves that make driving a bit of fun. Everybody's headlights are on, and there's a sign that says, "Pennsylvania's Maximum Speed Limit is Still 55 Miles An Hour." Nobody on this road is driving fifty-five miles an hour, despite the rain and the mist and the gathering darkness. We are, after all, in America now.

5:59 P.M.

Just outside Town Hill, Pennsylvania, the rain and the lightning and the closeness of the mountains have slowed traffic. We're traveling forty-five, maybe fifty, MPH, drivers getting jumpy as the occasional puddle causes a hydroplane. Cars have pulled over, flashers going at the side of the road, to wait for this storm cell to go by, while others, myself included, keep plugging along.

All Things Considered has just finished a story about the *Spruce Goose* and its possible future. Someone may actually try to get that beautiful monster in the air again. I've just passed a car spinning its wheels in a ditch. It's difficult not to want a flying boat in so much water as there is now in the Pennsylvania hills. I pull back on my steering wheel, like I would pull back on an airplane's stick, but nothing happens.

6:06 P.M.

I get off at Exit 29 for Breezewood, Everett, and Bedford. My intent, being an American traveler, is to visit McDonald's. And when I come to a stop I see for the first time how hard it really is raining. Although the wind coming off the car allowed me to keep a window open on the interstate, here (as I pass a bar that, in six-foot letters, says I will find Girls! Girls! Girls! inside) I have to close my windows tightly to keep from getting drenched.

Is there anything, any place or event or icon, more intimately American than McDonald's? Isn't McDonald's the place that bothers us in London and Syndey because of the way it signifies the export of a part of our culture that's fast and cheap and not really all that good for anyone, while at the same time we stand there ordering lunch, basking in the comfort of the familiar?

In this Pennsylvania McDonald's, which looks like every other McDonald's on the planet, I order two cheeseburgers, a large order of fries, and a thermos of coffee. This McDonald's is a cosmopolitan place—Asians, Hispanics, whites, and blacks, a great many people who have come off the highway to escape the rain and gain a bit of respite.

The man standing behind me—sandy-brown hair, a beard, about six feet tall—turns to his friends at the end of the line and says, "Two hours left." The tone of his voice carries both promise and miles already traveled. Because it's taken me two hours from D.C. to here, because I think he said he was going to Washington and I am going to warn him about the rain, the traffic, the cars in the ditches, I turn around and ask if he's heading east. He says no, he is traveling west like I am. We chuckle about the rain. "It's a parking lot out there right now," he says.

This man and I know what we share. We have come off a road that could have spilled us toward a ditch or worse. We have come off hours behind a wheel. Turning to this stranger and speaking, just to make small talk if nothing else, is a type of pleasure. Neither this man nor I would turn to a stranger on a city street and assume some context or community that makes us similar. But here, in this McDonald's, off this road, through this storm, this man and I realize the social definitions have changed. We are a part of the same community now. We do not take the time to sit and share our meal, but we could.

The young woman who takes my order is a freshman, maybe a sophomore, in high school. Very pleasant, willing to help, at times thoroughly flustered but constantly smiling. Standing next to her, a not very much older McDonald's manager, who understands every nuance of ordering and service, is slightly dismayed at so much success for her business. She and I smile at each other when my order goes awry, and I imagine she too has spent hours on some highway, that she too knows the comfort and succor we can find in the familiar and known routine of her work.

Like most highway travelers, I'm not going to eat my food in the McDonald's. I get my brown paper bag made of recycled paper, my thermos of fresh coffee, and in a couple of minutes I am back on Highway 70 heading west into America.

6:31 P.M.

Heading west on a Penn-Turnpike that's suddenly very congested and slow, sun breaking out, rain still falling though misting more, I learn something about mountain radio. I'm listening to Peter Frampton's "Do You Feel Like I Do?" a Sunday sermon, some easy listening tune called "With a Song in My Heart," and, way off in the distance, the Dire Straits, all competing for the same frequency. As I come around a curve, a different valley allows a different signal and a different song becomes prominent. All of it static. All of it wonderful.

But I discover a problem with my planning. I started this trip cross-country with twenty-one dollars in my pocket. Looking over my resources after parking lot A and my dinner at McDonald's, I realize I have fifteen dollars left with the Penn-Turnpike and the Chicago Toll Road in front of me.

7:05 P.M.

When the setting sun finds some room between the clouds, I find myself in picture-postcard America, in western Pennsylvania at the 126 mile marker. This is a land of steep and frequent valleys. The world here is one large deciduous forest, interrupted only briefly by cornfields or by cattle grazing. Of course, the Pennsylvania Turnpike interminably interrupts the picture, and perhaps this is a sad view, the pavement breaking the landscape. But the roads are steep and banked and twisty, and because the rain has left us, they're dry and fun to drive. I lean into the curves, forward in the stretch, wishing I were at Daytona or Indy.

A sign says, "Trucks Under 40 Miles Per Hour, Use Flashers," but nobody here is traveling forty miles an hour. Some of us are closer to eighty. The sun, through the mist, is just a bright disc in the sky, easy to look at. There's haze in the air ahead, and it's humid this late August. Soon will come September and October and the brilliant colors of fall, and then the hard snowfall of winter.

When the Allegheny Mountain Tunnel appears, a sign says, "Stay in lane. Do not cross center line." Inside the tunnel, I cannot resist two or three honks of the horn.

7:12 P.M.
I pass a sign that tells me the "Minimum Fine for Speeding in This State is $92.50." Almost by instinct, and certainly from habit, my foot comes off the accelerator, momentarily.

7:48 P.M.
My heart almost stops. Coming down the west side of the hill, thirty miles east of Pittsburgh, we come around a bend and into the best-placed speed trap I've seen. I hit the brakes instinctively, giving myself away as a transgressor, a scofflaw, somebody whose civil disobedience is poorly aimed. But the officer, for whatever reason, doesn't come out after me. Perhaps it is because I wasn't going that fast, only sixty-five miles an hour. Perhaps because he knows there's bigger fish on this road. After I pass the trap, a Mercedes followed by a BMW, both with CB antennas, both with mobile telephone antennas, go speeding by me. They knew where that cop was, of course, and I imagine they looked so prim going past him, so proper and well behaved. It's the type of justice that makes me want to smile and cry at the same time.

7:55 P.M.

I-70 and I-76 split. I-70 heads west off toward Wheeling, Columbus, Indianapolis, St. Louis, on into Kansas City, then Denver and beyond. It's tough for me to not take that road. I was born in Kansas City. I went to college in Columbia, Missouri, a town right on I-70 and halfway between Kansas City and St. Louis. It's tough not to want to go visit old apartments, old friends. I know the memories would disappoint me if I went to visit them, the way old homes or schools always fail to bend time quite enough, but the pull is strong and it's evening. Just the right time for fantasies, for imagining old friends and lovers still inhabiting the same apartments, that they would remember me and the time between us would disappear.

When you're driving alone on an interstate highway, listening to jazz ballads, you're feeling many miles from anywhere you've got a connection. Feeling not a part of any real community that's close to you, except the community of isolated vagabonds. Short hoppers and long trippers together. All of us breaking the law. All of us wanting to get somewhere—to be hugged, to be welcomed in, to be greeted. So memories of old places and old times can rise up and become real with the passing of a road sign that names the places you knew.

I stay on I-76, heading toward deeper memories than my college days, heading west toward Chicago.

8:47 P.M.

The sun has set. A half-moon shines toward the left side of my car, and the fog is settling thickly over western Pennsylvania. Pittsburgh is a memory fading back into the rainstorm. The Ohio border is twenty-two miles away.

There's something both odd and regular about traffic patterns tonight. The semis have disappeared. The roads have somehow widened with their absence, but there's also a void they leave behind. Relationships between highway drivers are built on size and speed, and those trucks have both. When the truckers take a break, those of us left to the road breathe a bit more fully, set the cruise control perhaps just a little bit faster. There's not so much or so many blocking our view. It's easy to feel a type of small when you can see the horizon.

From now until about ten o'clock the truckers will rest, eat dinner, walk about. They're required by law to take a break every eight hours, and perhaps this is the changing of the guard. By ten o'clock, however, there will be ten trucks for every car, and, even though I'm speeding now, I'll be the slowest thing on the road. The horizon will weigh one hundred tons and pass my sixty-five mph fast.

I used to own a CB radio—when everybody used to have a CB radio—and everyone crowded into Channel 19 saying, "Breaker, trucker!" We all asked for friends' and strangers' "20," even if we knew perfectly well where they were. We called out the mile markers, we basked in the opportunity to say "10-4" whether it was appropriate or not, and we gave voice to the gibberish of people too bored in cars and trucks by themselves, too desperately alone and needing to call out, if only to get somebody angry.

In my car this evening, however, I'm listening to a jazz station from Pittsburgh as my headlights illuminate the fog in odd and wonderful patterns—and I'm glad for the relative silence.

9:15 P.M.
I'm at the Gateway Tollbooth to the Pennsylvania Turnpike. In front of me is the breadth of Ohio. I pull over to the side, pour myself a fresh cup of coffee, and after the $6.50 toll realize my resources are down to $5.37.

9:17 P.M.
"Ohio Welcomes You."

9:18 P.M.

"Speed Above the Posted Limits Will Not Be Tolerated."

9:24 P.M.

I pass the first service station in Ohio, twin McDonald's and BP stations on both sides of the road, and I see a one-eyed car coming down the other side of the highway. Suddenly, my heart is filled with a small memory from high school.

There are people who have changed my life, and Holly Smith is one of them. I doubt she remembers me. We did not date each other for long. Our romance was neither torrid nor deep. But one early evening on Waukeegan Road in Lake Forest, Illinois, we passed a one-eyed car. I was driving. "Padiddle," she said. Then she leaned over and kissed me on the cheek. I asked her what "padiddle" meant, and she said it was just what you should do when you pass a car with only one working headlight, like lifting your feet when you pass over railroad tracks. I don't remember when or how we stopped seeing each other, but since then, every time I have seen a one-eyed car, I have thought of her. I have missed the warm feeling of her lips on the side of my face. She gave me a definition I still carry.

10:18 P.M.

Even though it's dark and there's only a half-moon playing peekaboo with scattered clouds, forty-three miles east of Cleveland it's easy to see the mountains have given way to the beginnings of flatlands. Geologically, I'm still a long, long way from the prairie, from the treeless ground I call home, but where I am is in every other respect Heartland America. When it's not the forest coming up to the roadside, it's farmland, still mostly corn.

As if on cue, the trucks have come back to the highway. Not the fleets that will come later into the evening, but certainly a good many more than earlier tonight. And I find myself wishing I'd chosen another route. Even at night these are busy roads. Hundreds of cars and trucks. Short hoppers and long haulers. Had I taken 64 West out of Virginia, across West Virginia and into Kentucky, and then up through Indiana, I'd be driving on those vast stretches of sparsely populated highway, the moon shining over riverbed farmland. Perhaps I would be reliving a night in Missouri, when I was much younger—a brilliant full-moon night when I drove with top and windows down, lights off, at nearly one hundred mph.

There is something that speaks to the American Romantic spirit about being on an open lonely road late at night, about finding that one light still burning at the cafe or motel. But to be on a turnpike late at night, to be merely one of one hundred cars, one of a hundred hundred cars, makes the trip seem more workmanlike, more like simply getting somewhere than an escapade in the art of traveling.

Here on the northern corridor the radio stations are clear, the rain has gone away, the speed limit in Ohio is sixty-five, and the miles fall away unnoticed, uncounted, and pretty much ignored. There's a complete and utter absence of community. At the BP station, all I did was insert my credit card. I pumped my gas, and the pump gave me a receipt. No human interaction required. The model of efficiency. Of course, I did stick my head in just to say hello and ask where the bathrooms were. But it is possible, now, to travel great distances unnoticed, uncounted, uncared for, unknown except to a network of machines. Faster, certainly, but also less engaged and less alive.

10:26 P.M.
The exit for Kent State University.

11:13 P.M.
At the 150 mile marker on the Ohio Turnpike I pass a sign that says Chicago is 320 miles in front of me. On this transcontinental scale, that's a distance I can taste.

Chicago is an emotional place for me, a place of history and desire. From fifth grade into college I walked the city and suburb streets there. I came to understand real music. I came to understand violence. I came to understand the Italian beef sandwich. I've been stuck at O'Hare for three days in snow. And I've been in love at the lake shore. It's a city where simple landmarks carry a personal weight.

I'll not be stopping there, but I will certainly slow.

12:08 A.M.

Coming up to Exit 7, I pass the first triple-tandem truck I've seen this voyage. It is followed by two more. These are flatland cruisers, moving faster than my own seventy mph. I don't know how many tons of food, stereos, Barbie dolls, and blue jeans are passing me here, but their simple force on the road is enough to make my own car shudder. In the oceans, dolphins play in the bow waves of the giant tankers and cruisers. They leap and dart and provide some type of proof that nature is not only big fish eating little fish, proof there is still some room enough for play. But on the interstate the bow wave of the semi is proof a big enough engine can pull anything behind it, push anything out of its way.

Exit 7 is Route 250, a little road heading toward Sandusky and Noah. Six miles north of the exit I pull into a Ramada Inn. I've passed other hotels, each promoting sauna or hot tub availabilities, each letting me know what movie channel I would find on their televisions, but I managed to make a reservation at this Ramada, so I feel a type of obligation. When I was in graduate school I spent my summers and then the full seasonal cycle working as a night auditor for hotels. Night auditors are front desk clerks who work from eleven at night until seven in the morning, adding up that previous day's business, arranging that day's bank deposit, fending off the drunks, and welcoming the tired in the middle of the night. I've turned people away because someone called and asked me to hold a room, and I've had that person not show up.

There's a woman behind the front desk. She is young, just

graduated from high school, it seems, maybe twenty years old, the night auditor. I tell her my name; she brings me a room key. She imprints my credit card; I sign the form. We get to talking about the hotel. This hotel doesn't have the Jacuzzi suites the others in the area do. The manager even sent back all the dirty movies. "A conservative manager, eh?" I ask. She says, "Very much so."

We talk for a few minutes. I want to talk because the only words I've spoken since I left Maureen have been business words. She wants to talk because it's a slow night at the Ramada. We share some stories about working the night shift. I tell her about the married couple who cheated on each other, and how they both showed up with their flings at the hotel on the same night, and how I put them in adjoining rooms just for fun. She tells me about the conventions, the mass emigration of linen and towels, the people snuck into rooms. Our stories do not surprise each other; we each have our own version. But we make the point of sharing, of adding something to this night in the progress of so many still to come, of making a connection, and it feels good to talk.

In the course of our conversation, she goes on to tell me she's getting married, and when she gets married her wedding night will be spent at a competitor's hotel down the street—a place with hot tubs and movies. We both laugh.

Finally I drive around to door B, head down to room 114. When I get there and flip on the television, to defeat my feelings of being apart from the recognizable and familiar routines of home, to check in with the known patterns of electronic drama and comedy and news, I discover the world has turned upside down. That there is a different type of community interest. Mikhail Gorbachev has been placed under house arrest. There is a committee leadership in the Soviet Union. The bombs are in question. Progress has shifted direction. No one knows the intent or meaning of the new men in charge. The original players have been taken off the stage. And suddenly people are checking home.

I call Maureen. She says hurry home.

Day Two

8:10 A.M.

Monday morning now, I am packed and about to leave the hotel. It is a quieting morning. I've been told there are rain showers in the area, and it's clear network news is fully up to speed. President Bush is speaking from Kennebunkport about the replacement of leadership in the Soviet Union. There are analysts and anchors and reporters, historians, experts. They tell me where Boris Yeltsin is and what he's doing, what they think he should or must do next. They tell me where Gorbachev is, what his captors have said about him. And they spend considerable time forecasting the future of arms control, human rights, trade agreements, democracy, and communism, life as we know it.

Today, however, I cannot sit in front of my television and wait for illumination. Today I cannot walk to my college office and discuss our collective fear of the potential with intelligent women and men. Today I go back to the highways, to getting glimpses of homes and shops and farms and towns and the places where lives are invested and lived, but I cannot stop to visit even with them. I must get home as fast as mechanics and law will allow. I will have radio news. I will have my memory and imagination. I do not believe the world will end today. But I realize it might. I'm three hundred miles from Chicago, a full day's drive from there to get back to Maureen and Kate.

8:39 A.M.

I'm pulling away from the High-Miler, a convenience store and Shell station. I have a full tank of gas from last night so I don't fill up, but I am missing the other essentials of highway driving—doughnuts, soda, potato chips, things that crumble and fall in my lap—so I have to make this stop.

A brown-haired man with a moustache, the clerk, and I get to talking about baseball. How this comes up I'm not really sure. He's a Pirates fan. I'm rooting for the White Sox and Cubs this year, as always. We talk about dreams, failed dreams, how the Cubs every year seem to lead the way and then go on vacation before the rest of the league does. At one point we're even talking about a Cubs and White Sox World Series. How lovely it would be to see something like that. He says it'll never happen, of course. "But look at Missouri," I say. "They did it just a couple years ago."

Behind him and over his head there is a small television and news of the world. The man and I quiet every few minutes, each time the announcer begins a sentence with "We have just learned . . ."

I ask this clerk how many people buy a hot dog at 8:30 in the morning. The hot dogs here are on one of those roller beds, being slowly turned and turned and turned into oblivion, and I get the disturbing impression it's impossible to date them. I bet a hot dog could turn on one of those roller beds for seven years and still look like it did when it came out of the package. The man says, "Oh, you wouldn't believe the hot dogs we sell—any time of the day."

I dawdle in the store longer than I should, captivated by the televised insistence of world upheaval, then manage to leave.

As I pull away and head south back toward the turnpike, the sun is coming out. The cornfield to my right looks about a week from harvest. There are beans to my left. The morning traffic has begun. I pass a billboard for Firearms Unlimited, Inc. The billboard shows a handgun.

Somewhere around me, just to the north, although I can't see it, is Lake Erie. I want to visit Lake Erie. I want to see if Lake Erie is as clean as recent reports or as dirty as I remember. And I want to rekindle whatever connection it is human beings have with large deep water. To watch the sailboats leaving anchor, the freighters weighing in, the methods of commerce and pleasure and transport on water. To relax and let small angers in me fade. To let the waters subsume my fears and isolation.

8:40 A.M.
I pull up and get my ticket to the Ohio Turnpike, once again head
west. I cashed a check at the Ramada. I'm ready to go.

8:54 A.M.
I am no longer surrounded by the mountains of Pennsylvania.
Ohio, I see, is the start of Farmland America. Corn is the crop of
choice. The land is flat and rich and fertile. I engage the cruise control, and it's nice to sit back. Radio news is recounting the supposed chronology of the coup. The interviews of experts have been
arranged for later in the morning.

Perhaps we've all just gone crazy, I think. The entire planet is
holding its breath today, and, at the High-Miler, I bought two long-
john caramel-icing doughnuts, a package of six little powdered
round doughnuts, four large Sprites, a thermos of coffee. Radio
news pauses for rock and roll, the sale of chewing gum and acne
pads. I'm eating doughnuts while driving on cruise control in
America.

9:17 A.M.
Eastbound traffic has its lights on. Southwest of the interstate the
clouds have deepened to a steel-gray slate. The storms are coming
again. In this part of the world, where what comes from earth and
sky can give or take our lives, I'm struck by how shallow the distance is between storm cloud and earth. How fragile the atmosphere. And how dynamic. On the East Coast today there is a hurricane—Hurricane Bob. Hurricane Bob should hit New England this
afternoon and bring its storm surge with it. Tonight the news from
the Soviet Union will be interrupted to show scenes of flooded
homes, trees bending in the terrific wind while announcers esti-
mate the cost of catastrophe.

I've been in tornadoes. I've been in hail and wind and lightning
and heavy thunder. I have smelled the ozone of a lightning strike

too close to where I hid. That's what you get from growing up midwestern. I've been in ground blizzards where I couldn't see my hand in front of me because of the snow in the crazy huge wind, while looking up I could make my way by stars. But I do not understand a hurricane. I've been close to one or two. But the persistence of that wind is beyond my tornado comparisons. I cannot imagine what people in Boston, or Moscow, are saying today as they wait, what they could say in a common language, and I feel lonely because of it.

9:27 A.M.
The rain comes. I'm at Exit 4, and a black Mercedes whizzes by me. I was in the left-hand lane as it approached, saw it flash its lights Autobahn-style to get me to move over, and my first instinct was to say, "No. I'm speeding. You don't need to speed faster than I'm speeding." But then, I know if I were in his car, I'd be doing that too.

10:11 A.M.
Again the rain has slowed traffic down to forty miles an hour. At least I'm not in mountains now. These roads are relatively straight, relatively safe when you really can't see. Grayness covers everything today. The trees look gray. The grass looks gray. The road looks gray. Farm animals, cars and trucks, road signs all have shades of gray hiding in them, hovering at the corners. In another light this countryside could define something pleasant and real about what we would like to believe our nation trusts, the trees and farmsteads, that herd of beef cattle less than thirty yards to my right watching traffic and, perhaps, wondering why we go so far to simply repeat our habits. But image making is closed today due to reality. Our speed slows to zero. Both lanes completely stop. Something up in front of us, obviously, has gone wrong.

I strain my eyes to see between the cars in front of me, wondering what's happened, feeling a minuscule connection with the Russians and New Englanders whose routine has also gone to hell, then notice something right under my nose. The car in front of me, the blue-gray Chevrolet Celebrity wagon with a Sears cargo carrier on top and two children's bicycles on a rack, is wearing Minnesota plates. That's my state! I think. Maybe I know these people! I laugh a little bit out loud, recognizing the hope that comes from connections, and I wave at these people when I pass them a little farther down the road. I trust they will notice my plate, my highway identification, as well.

10:41 A.M.

Just a stumble from the Indiana border and my car turns sixty thousand miles. For some reason this is exciting, and I slow down to watch the numbers turn.

12:05 P.M.

I'm pulling out of the Bob's Big Boy at a turnpike service plaza, feeling the Big Boy is what I expected. It's one story tall, filled with pay phones and arcade games. There's a gift shop (closed) and a cafeteria-style restaurant—the type where you wonder if the cooks really cook or just dish up meals delivered hot from some giant industrial kitchen. In a way I felt good walking in here; I knew what to expect. In another context I like some adventure in dining, some new taste or combination. But today the missiles could fall, and I am still some distance from home.

I pulled into the Big Boy because of the rain. It began to peter out as I passed Exit 121, Indiana 1, at Howe and LaGrange. But then it came back. First, a fine mist. Then, sometimes harder. Sometimes a lot harder. Then sheets of it. Sheets falling from the sky, sheets exploding off the sides and wheels of trucks and cars. A dirty rain in a darkening day. I could see the clouds lightening and dimming in the distance.

Although it's early, the rain made this rest stop necessary to clear my brain. I can focus on the road only so long before it begins to disappear. I bought a fresh tank of gas. In the Big Boy I ordered a cheeseburger and french fries. I knew it was coming, the absurd cost of these things, but I could not get over my anger. I asked the cashier what he thought about torturing hostages, but he didn't get my point.

I took the food to my car. For a short time I sat there, behind the steering wheel, eating and listening to radio news. There's a hurricane hitting New England and a coup in the Soviet Union, but the news people are having trouble filling time. No one has died in the storm; no homes have been lost. Those who lead and those who follow in Russia are wondering what to do next. All the announcers and experts can do is wait, predict, talk about what and who they saw their last visit. Even National Public Radio seems to be in a holding pattern.

12:30 P.M.
An odometer reading—60,101.8. I pass a sign that says, "Entering CST." So now my car clock is right. It's 11:30. And my wristwatch is wrong. I take it off and fumble trying to set it while driving.

11:46 A.M.
Forty miles east of Chicago and the sky darkens again quickly, ominously. In front of me I can see the wall of rain I'm approaching. It's time for lights and wipers, for a seat belt tightened. This is beginning to be a dismal drive, I think. Whatever romance I had imagined or hoped for is fading into an oppressive gray of sky and road and mist and rain.

12:13 P.M.
The rain has paused. The skies are still clouded over with smog and soot and the general effluence from the Gary steelworks. I'm in the north side of Gary, Indiana, the industrial side, about as close to a vision of hell as the United States can come up with. Even Lake Michigan, off to my right, brought under my feet by canals, is

wasted and filthy here. Perhaps, once, this was a scene of the American industrial might and promise. The smokestacks and factories, the barges and conveyors, the paving over of everything living, and a gross consumption for the transformation of resources— perhaps people smiled when they looked at this. But today, to me, this is mortal sin. In Gary, I even find it difficult to imagine my prairie home, the broad, open farmlands, the blanketing snowfalls, because the prairie has never threatened towns like Gary. It's always the other way around.

12:27 P.M.
Welcome to Chicago! I'm on Highway 90, driving by corroded grain bins, a faded brick elevator. Steel everywhere. The refuse of industry. On the radio is a State Department briefing about the overthrow of Gorbachev. All they can say is they're waiting to see what happens. They're concerned about this change. No shit, guys, I think. It's a gloomy day in Moscow. It's a gloomy day in south Chicago. It's a gloomy day for the world.

1:07 P.M.
I am fifty feet in front of the tollbooth on I-90 northwest of Chicago, just south of O'Hare. And not only is it raining hard, but I am in the thing that defines the Chicago expressways. A traffic jam.

When I imagined this trip, I imagined side trips here. Lunch at a restaurant I once favored with a friend who edits a journal. Or maybe just parking in front of a house my family once owned, just to watch who comes in and out and how. But today I think my memories are better faced alone. Old homes, old schools, they all require explanation, a context shifting, if anyone else is going to understand. I once visited with a family who lived in a home my family once lived in, and I tried to explain what it was like for us. What games we played. The events we shared. The family was polite about it. But they were dumb and I was mute.

This day has gone to hell, I think, and Chicago is ugly in this rain. I pay my toll and roll my window tightly. I speed just a little bit more to get me home.

2:20 P.M.

I am in Wisconsin now. Chicago and northern Illinois fell into the rain and mist of this day without event, without drama. I took a more western road than I had planned, to get me home faster, to avoid the exits that used to lead me home.

These miles cannot go fast enough! Radio news continues to say nothing real about the disintegration of the Soviet hierarchy, the almost certain destruction of perestroika and glasnost, and I am stuck in a metal box with wheels, trying to span a nation before sleep comes over me again. Today, my imagination is not turning over the idea of community or context anymore. The whole thing just seems silly. My body is in a car traversing Wisconsin. My heart is on the Minnesota and North Dakota border. My mind is in Moscow. I've just ignored the state of Illinois.

Most of us don't think of our states very much. Where I live, North Dakota and Minnesota bump into each other so well it's hard to notice the bridge over the Red River. At the Illinois and Wisconsin border, there were no gates or booths or officials. Just a sign, easily ignored. The whole idea of family, friends, colleagues, neighborhood, regional community, national community, international, and then planetary consciousness seems both affirmed and defeated today; I can't get a grip on which. Last night, that Ramada desk clerk and I talked with each other, shared small parts of ourselves in the middle of a lonely night. But does she vote like I vote? Does she value what I do? Would we be friends? Could we share our sympathies and rages?

There is a way in which driving in a car across the United States parallels what's going on in the Soviet Union, the ethnic and philosophic bias of one group for or against the other. Each border I cross is there for a reason. They help us define ourselves and our culture, community, context. We depend on them for law. And we ignore them too much.

4:02 P.M.

I was listening to trombone music from Berlin on National Public Radio, just before *All Things Considered* came on, and now I'm driving I-94 between the short hills and bluffs and valleys that surround the Wisconsin Dells. At the 99 mile marker there are an ambulance and police cars. General havoc. Fire trucks. Delayed traffic. There's been an accident—a Chevy Blazer and what appears to be a truck have collided and flipped. Eastbound traffic is at a standstill.

4:33 P.M.

The sun! The unmitigated, wonderful sun! The unobstructed sun—except for soft white cotton-ball clouds. The rays look like those in paintings you get with seagulls or something religious, and I'm loving every minute of it. I put my sunglasses on for the few hours I've got before sunset. And instantly my heart grows softer and more curious. God! I want to stop here. I want to get to know someone well. I don't know why, but I'm feeling a type of ownership or membership here. A Maine plate goes by on a little red car. Maine's getting a hurricane today. But I am not in Maine. And I am not in the Soviet Union. I am in a beautiful late Wisconsin afternoon—long, low clouds, brilliant sunshine.

5:33 P.M.

I'm at the Northfield exit. Still about 120 miles from St. Paul. I'm passing farms of Christmas trees. I notice in the forests here the rolling hills dotted with meadows. And I notice in the forests that a shift is taking place, deciduous trees giving way to conifers, leafy things giving way to evergreens. Red farm buildings. White farmhouses. Cattle grazing. An occasional satellite dish out near the barn. Even here, the news can come from outer space.

There are few cars or trucks on the highway this afternoon. A contrast to the industrial corridor from Chicago through Pittsburgh and into Washington. There's simply more space to breathe here. More space to feel at home. I feel so good I shout "Yippie" out the window I've rolled down. Really.

6:31 P.M.

Thirty-three miles east of Minnesota, still. There's not a cloud in the sky. The fields are a luminous green. The air is still and cool. It's become a perfect late summer afternoon. Norman Rockwell would have loved it.

6:49 P.M.

Twelve miles from Minnesota, half the planet from what scares me speechless, three hot-air balloons off in the western distance hang just so beautifully. Make that four balloons, five balloons, scattered left and right. Reds and greens and blues and white. Stripes vertical. Stripes horizontal. What a way to spend the day. I know it must be lovely. Maureen has been up in a balloon; I helped inflate it. But I could never go up in one. I don't mind airplanes, but I fear there's too strong a pull in a balloon, too much space to lean into. I'd want to lean over and just keep leaning.

When I get to the St. Croix River, the balloons are directly above me. In front of me are three ultralight airplanes doing lazy figure eights over the interstate. There are pleasure boats out on the water, sailboats moored off to the right. My odometer reads 60,559.3. Welcome to Minnesota!

8:09 P.M.

The sun is just setting below the horizon. There appears to be a thunderhead a good way up in the western distance, though overhead the sky is clear. It's that odd moment in highway travel when I've got my lights on and I'm wearing my sunglasses too. In the dips between the hills you need the light. When you get to the top of the hill, the setting sun is too brilliant for the naked eye.

Off to my right is a series of road construction tractors. Beyond them, the hills of idyllic Minnesota. So much of this country is picture-postcard type, I think. So much of it is so open. It's difficult, once you live here, once you taste living here, to imagine life in a more crowded, less human, more disconnected place. The sense of community in the rural parts of America is stronger than it is in the urban areas. More expansive. At its best more inclusive. It is certainly more generous.

I know the sun is setting over the Dakotas. I'm only a couple miles west of Minneapolis, but here I discover my imagination can reach toward home—where I know what Maureen and Kate are looking at when they stand at a window, the temper and timbre of the light they see. In front of me is Alexandria, where I'll make the obligatory stop at the McDonald's to see if there's anyone I know. Then it's home to Maureen and Kate and my dog. To the mail that's built up after a week's vacation. To the routine of my life.

I chuckle as the exit for Monticello comes and goes. You can see Jefferson's Monticello from my parents' farm, where this drive began, and here I am passing it again.

9:07 P.M.
The same half-moon that chased me last night is again at the driver's side window. There are deep purples in the western sky. The sun has long set, but the twilight lingers. In fields, occasionally, I see the brilliant lamps of farmers harvesting despite the darkness. I'm in a land of beans and grains, most of which are already in. Trees are much scarcer here. I'm approaching Sauk Centre, and it's evident that very soon, geographically, psychologically, philosophically, and politically, I'll be on the American prairie.

9:46 P.M.
I make the necessary stop at the Alexandria McDonald's. I have $1.56 to spend, which only gets me a milk shake, but in telling that story to the short blonde-haired girl at the counter, who looks as though she's eleven years old, she takes pity on me and hands me a small package of McDonaldland Cookies as well, for free. I tell her I love her, which I do.

10:54 P.M.

Clay County! Almost home.

11:18 P.M.

I'm at Exit 1A—the intersection of I-94 and 75. The odometer says
60,818.5 miles, and I am no longer on the interstate highway system. I have finished my trip. I've come home to Moorhead, Minnesota, just this side of Fargo. At the beginning I said I wanted to
see what could be learned or felt on a trip like this. I hadn't counted
on the rain closing off my imagination, politics closing off my hope.
But I am home again, and better for the trip.

I've made it home. My car did not break down. I did not have a
wreck. I didn't pick up a hitchhiker who revealed either truth or a
knife. I met no personal crisis with bravery or cowardice. I just
drove home. By myself. Alone with some certain memories, some
certain desires.

My dog meets me at the door, happy to see me. I take off my
coat, walk upstairs and into my daughter's room; Kate has long
since been asleep. I look at her for a short while, touch my hand to
her cheek. Maureen turns over in bed when I come into our bedroom, asks me how the trip has been and whether I've got notes for
the essay I've told her I'm going to write. Yes, I say. I've got some
notes. Memories mostly, I tell her. And curiosities, I say. Like wondering who it was I passed, who it was that passed me. Like the
huge differences between Washington and Sandusky, between
Moorhead and Moscow. Like which cells in my brain held my
memory of Holly Smith until I saw the one-eyed car. But mostly, I
tell her, my notes are about coming home.

Good, she says. We hug each other until we are both asleep.

DUST AND GRAVEL, BEAUTY AND DREAMS

TEN O'CLOCK IN THE MORNING—A BRIGHT, SUN-FILLED SKY overhead with just a hint of some clouds, an idea that something larger might still develop—and I am standing on a bridge that spans the Klondike River in Canada's Yukon Territory looking down into the water, looking for fish, wondering how long it takes for the rainfall to become river water and pass this place, and wondering how long it takes this river water to reach the ocean. I have never stood here before this morning. The bridge is the beginning of the Dempster Highway, a road I have never traveled. But I know this bridge, and I know this road.

Thousands of miles away from where I am standing this morning, I asked a simple question. How far away can I drive? Where do the roads finally end? If you ask a question the right way, or the wrong way enough, you begin to hear stories. As I took my question to maps and tourists and explorers, I began to hear stories about this road, this small gravel path that in summer ends in a delta town called Inuvik, and in winter uses river ice until it ends in Tuktoyaktuk, on the shores of the Beaufort Sea, the Arctic Ocean.

And the stories were wonderful, dangerous and thrilling and beautiful. I imagined myself in every single one of them.

Just a few minutes before this moment, not a hundred yards away, at a gas station and restaurant and lodge called the Klondike Corner, a man in a government uniform walked up to me as I filled the Jeep with gas.

"Minnesota, eh?" he said, after looking at my license plates, more statement than question.

"Yep," I said.

"I fought fires there," he said, smiling broadly. Then he told me he fought the Yellowstone fire and the Fox Lake fire. He told me there is a fire, maybe going to be a big one, over in Alaska now. He said he dispatched the tankers out of Dawson City just yesterday. He said he liked Minnesota, and that he'd like to go back there someday just to look around. He told me stories, and when he left we shook hands and it occurred to me I'd never heard his name.

On the bridge, looking down, I can see the Klondike River is shallow, very clear and very fast. The stories I know from history tell me this is one of the gold rush rivers. The stories I know from yesterday tell me the mining continues. But this river is not why I am here. Turning, and looking north, I can see the Dempster rise gently, a straight path between lodgepole pines. In the distance, I can see the Tombstone Mountains, sharp and jagged.

Seven hundred thirty-seven kilometers. Four hundred fifty-seven miles. Nearly all of it gravel. North of the Arctic Circle, a lot of the gravel is tire-slashing broken black shale. Gas only at Eagle Plains, the halfway point, and then again at Fort McPherson and Inuvik. Three times across the continental divide. Four times over mountain ranges, then down into river valleys and muskeg. Ptarmigan, hare, siksik, red fox, muskrat, beaver, martin, wolf, arctic fox, lynx, Barren Ground grizzly bear, black bear, moose, Barren Ground caribou from the Bluenose and Porcupine herds, wolverine, hoary marmot, Dall sheep, and, just offshore, beluga whale. And this doesn't even begin to name the plants or the millions of birds who migrate through here. Very few people. Little rescue for the stupid or the poorly prepared. Space enough to breathe. When I leave the bridge, start the Jeep, and crest the first small hill, the mountains become a kind of promise or possibility. This is the last road in North America.

A plume of dust, bright white and thick in the summer sunshine, kicks up from my tires. The sound of driving on gravel becomes background noise. The roadway, built on a berm much like a railway to counter the muskeg and permafrost, heads toward the mountains. Very quickly I come upon a blue van with a flat tire. I slow, to offer what I can, and discover no one is near. I do not know if the spare is already on one of the wheels.

The Tombstone Mountains get their name not from catastrophe, not from any lost party of men and women who perished, but simply from the way they look. Dark igneous rock, the remains of a granite batholith, sharp faces rising fast out of the surrounding landscape, broken tops, they look like grave markers stacked up against some invisible wall.

I know from guidebooks, the ease of reading back in Dawson, coffee at my elbow and the Yukon River at my feet, that these mountains have never been glaciated. The ice sheets never covered them during the last ice age. The mountains in Alaska blocked most of the moisture, and there simply wasn't enough snow for glaciers to form. This means this part of the world became a refuge for wildlife, both plant and animal. And it means the great scraping and smoothing of the ice never happened here.

The mountains look different from the Rockies. The Rockies are old in the way that somebody's grandfather might be old. These mountains are old like a *Tyrannosaurus rex*. The Dempster goes up into the mountains, sometimes winding, sometimes dead straight. Sometimes there's just a minor embankment between the roadway and the muskeg; sometimes the drop-offs can be forty, fifty, as much as one hundred feet or more. Dangerous terrain in the best of times. Fireweed, a bright-pink plant that enjoys border ground, grows along the side of the highway with arctic cotton and gives, at least to me, the impression that some garden club has come out and decorated the highway—a long gray corridor of crushed rock, pretty pink-and-white flowers along the sides, and then the greens of the summer tundra.

Looking at the mountains, then the roadway, then the deep, shadowed valleys, then the mountains made different and new by a turn in the road and a fresh angle of light—every mile or kilometer is a source and then history of wonder and spectacle. Every minute I do not stop the Jeep, step out, and begin a hike toward some lake or ridge is a minute conflicted. It is not possible to be everywhere. It is not possible to explode into landscape.

Soon enough, though, I find myself stopping.

At the Tombstone Mountain campground, the first one on the road, the government runs an interpretative center. Two women, college age or perhaps just a bit older, both with brown hair but one with trendy blonde streaks, work in an old wooden building with a porch and happily offer advice and information to those who stop. Nearly everyone does. On the porch, amidst maps and nature posters and reports of the road's condition, there is a board where travelers can list their wildlife sightings. Today's list reads: grizzly bear, black bear, ptarmigan, moose, marmot, eagle, falcon, owl.

Inside the hut, another pair of women, in their later fifties or early sixties, are telling their story of driving back down the Dempster.

"Two flats," one tells me as I walk in. "Two flats, one right after the other. We got the first one changed, and maybe drove another half mile before the other one went."

"Black shale," says the other one. "North of the Arctic Circle the road is all black shale. Tires just can't take it. You're driving up? How many spares have you got?"

From the looks of them—bright smiles, dirt on the forearms, and grease on their jeans—they are not telling me a disaster story.

This is an adventure, trouble in the wilderness, and they have survived.

When the women leave ("Two flats!" I hear them tell someone in the gravel parking lot. "We had two flats . . . ") I ask the clerk with the blonde streaks about a hike to a waterfall that I had seen described in one of the guidebooks. Only a little more than a mile round-trip from the road, it sounds like a good way to breathe. I'm pretty sure I've already passed it—my car does not measure kilometers, I tell her—but I'd like to double back and find it if she can give me a landmark.

The clerk smiles at me. "That's not such an easy hike," she says. "I tried it myself a month ago. It was bushwhacking the whole way—really thick brush."

"Really?" I ask, disappointed.

"Yeah," she says. "And even if you wanted to do that, I wouldn't recommend it."

"Why?"

"There's two grizzly bears down there now."

"Oh," I say. "Good enough for me."

Walking back to the parking lot, I discover inertia can be a physical sensation. The body at rest, or in this case at a rest stop, tends to remain at rest. And there is a large part of me that wants to stop here, to set up a tent here and sit very still to watch the clouds and rain and sunlight move over the mountains. There is a large part of me that wants to learn this one small and particular and thus infinite place. The body in motion, though, is more than just an abstract wish. The call of the next valley, the next lake or river, the next bend in the road, is compelling and more than enough to turn me back toward the Jeep and its ignition.

Up to speed and heading north again, I find the rains moving in. Not thunderstorms. Nothing dramatic. Just showers. The valleys become gray with mist. The sky becomes gray with clouds. As the road crosses small hills and passes, the air is cold and windy. The road is no longer dry and dusty. It's gray with slime and muck.

I pass an emergency airstrip—the highway straight enough and wide enough, for long enough, that a small plane can land, an air ambulance, I suppose—yet with the fog I know it would be impossible for a plane to land this morning.

Though even with the rain, with the grayness, it is impossible to look at a landscape like this and not begin to feel that this is a huge place. I know, for example, from books and signs that I've been following the Tintina Trench, a rift valley that runs pretty much from Montana straight to north of Dawson and then into Alaska. The Tintina Trench, a possible extension of the Rocky Mountain Trench, changed the course of the Yukon River when the trench was filled with ice-age glaciers. And I know that these days sandhill cranes follow the trench on their migrations. But neither of these facts has anything to do with a faster heartbeat as the road turns a corner and the sun comes back out and the world seems so damn big and varied that I could never know anything true at all.

On the road there is always the promise of more.

Some hours up the roadway, I don't know how many, I come upon a man sitting on a lawn chair behind a van along the side of the Ogilvie River. The day has become sunny and warm. The river, broad and shallow and braided and tumbling over polished rocks, makes little noise. The valley here is broad enough to not feel close, but mountains rise to the east and west.

I slow and pull up a short way behind him. As far as I can tell, his tires are fine and he does not seem to be in trouble. This place, I decide, seems as good as any for fishing. As I unpack my rod and boots the man and I wave at each other. I look at the river for a few minutes, trying to figure out a good place to get in, and when I turn back I see the man has walked up to me. White hair, white beard, he swats at mosquitoes with a handkerchief.

"Lots of horsepower," he says, pointing at the Jeep. His accent is unmistakably German.

"Yes," I say.

"Good for this road," he says.

"Yes," I say.

"Salmon," he says. "They come up this river?"

"No," I say, mostly sure. "This river goes north, to the Arctic Ocean. Not west, or south, to the Pacific."

He pauses, and I assume it's to translate my English onto his German map of the Yukon. "OK."

He watches me tie a fly onto the end of my line.

"This river," he says. "This river, this road. Very, very nice." Each *very* he hits hard and slow.

"Yes," I say to him. "It is."

I fish for half an hour, maybe a little more, and watch two grayling rise and dance before I pull them in and let them go. But I leave early, because I've been told a story, and I'm close to the place.

Two hundred and twenty-something kilometers from the Klondike Corner, there is a small path leading east from the Dempster. It's unmarked—just two tire ruts heading into some woods toward the river. Yesterday, at the tourist information center in Dawson, when I asked about good places to go fishing, good places to spend time even if the fish weren't hungry, an Inuit woman took me aside and told me about this spot. "My grandmother," she said, "wanted to be buried with some rocks from this place."

Even looking for it, I pass it the first time by, not recognizing the trail. When I am certain I've gone too far, I double back, find it, and turn off the road. Fifty yards—maybe not even that much—of small trees and bushes, and then the trail breaks onto the stones and banks of the Ogilvie River. I drive the Jeep to the water's edge and get out.

A small waterfall here, really a small series of steps and cascades, and some back current that swirls to make a kind of whirlpool where I'm told the fish hold at the bottom and wait for food, or flies. This is a tremendously beautiful place. I fish for a while and don't catch a single one. Then I put the rod away and simply sit on the bank to watch. I am invisible to the roadway here, and the road is invisible to me. I lean back and close my eyes, wanting to only listen, and perhaps to drift into the warm comfort of a half sleep. But at every small noise I find myself looking. Bear? No. Close the eyes again. Snap. Bear? No. I know it's the wrong time of the year, but this is the place where the Porcupine Caribou herd moves on its way to or from the Arctic National Wildlife Refuge. This is the place where there are more animals than I have names for, and it is possible at this small place on the river to imagine I am the only person on earth.

Eventually, and almost reluctantly, I find myself back in the Jeep, heading north until I stop again, this time at the Eagle Plains Hotel, the halfway point on the Dempster Highway. Single story, long and narrow, the exterior made of corrugated steel or wood, the Eagle Plains Hotel does not give an outside appearance of comfort. Just to the south of the main building is the gas station and maintenance shop, a few small pumps for gasoline and diesel, a garage for tire and engine repair. Massive road-building machines are parked near the garage. The gravel parking lot is both mud and dust. The few cars are filthy. Mosquitoes thick and insistent. Off the north end of the hotel, a collection of tents and campers, canoes and kayaks, strapped to the tops of cars and pickup trucks, and the sound of healthy laughter.

Eagle Plains is on a broad ridge or plateau, and looking east from the step in front of the hotel I can see green tundra grass and willows, rolling hills and mountains in the distance—snow in the valleys. Above them to the north, clear sky and cotton-ball clouds. Above them to the south, a massive storm cell, rain and grayness in the distance.

For dinner tonight, chicken, mashed potatoes, a glass of beer, and then another. Satellite radio from Vancouver tells me what movies I can see downtown, or which pizza place will deliver the hottest pie. Satellite television is beamed into each hotel room. And it's all a pleasant if not disconcerting fantasy. A full menu in the restaurant, a well-stocked hotel bar, television and radio that seem so familiar. The staff, without exception, is eager to help and to be pleasant. If you didn't know any better, you wouldn't think about every drop of water here being trucked up to holding tanks. If you didn't know any better, you wouldn't think the electricity is made on-site.

When I pulled up to the hotel, I went looking for the surveyor's pin that I had read was here—a marker for the Canadian Gravity Standardization Project. I don't really know what that is, but it sounded too good not to find and touch. I knew it was somewhere near pipes outside the gas station. On my way there, I see a truck pull out of the tire repair bay and another truck pull right in. I walk in to ask the mechanic if he knows where the gravity pin is, and say hello to the driver whose tire is the current project.

"Having fun?" I ask.

"Oh, yeah," he says, smiling.

"Just one?"

"Two," he says. "I lost them both at the same place."

I find the pin and stare at it for a while, then am driven inside by the mosquitoes. In my hotel room I shower, get in bed, then get back up again. My mind knows it's late, very late, and yet it is light outside, even with the approaching storm. I'm restless. The only thing I want is to get on the highway and to be driving, to feel the miles or kilometers leap from beneath the wheels and into my legs and my heart. Being still somehow doesn't seem right.

Well after midnight and the sky is still bright. The storm isn't here yet, but I can tell it's getting closer. I'm reluctant to close the hotel room curtains. Reluctant to stop looking. I rest and then get up and go to the window. I rest again, then get up and go to the window. Finally, I rest and sleep.

IN THE MORNING, the sun has come out, the sky is bright, the mountains and the hills that fall away and rise again to every side are a deep, rich shade of green, and the breeze is a gentle one. The road itself, rutted and unevened by the rains and the traffic, is nothing less than thrilling as it follows a high ridge north. There is no other traffic, not a single other person within sight or imagination, and the white plume of dust behind the Jeep seems like decoration. In every sense, this is a fine morning in the Canadian Arctic.

Quickly, though, I find myself pulling off the road into a gravel parking lot, and smiling.

There are places on this planet that hold an odd and special power. Simply being there does something to our sense of success, of going beyond the mundane, of having done something real. The top of Everest is such a place, as is the Great Wall of China. Crossing the equator would fit, as would a day at Machu Picchu or the Bay of Fundy. Somehow these places wiggle their way into our imaginations when we are children, grab hold of some part of our desire, and never leave. We look for them on maps, find ourselves reading about them in waiting rooms and coffee shops. "I've always wanted to go there," we say. And if we are lucky, we go.

In front of me now, at the edge of the gravel roadway, is a sign. 66 degrees, 33 minutes north. The Arctic Circle. According to the OED, in 1556 a man named Robert Record wrote in his book *The Castle of Knowledge* that: "The Arctike circle is the greattest of all those circles whiche do always appear, and toucheth the Horizonte in only one pointe. . . . All the starres that bee within this circle nother rise nother set." This, according to the scholars, is the first time the words *Arctic Circle* were used as a phrase in English. (Chaucer gets credit for *Arctic* in 1391.) The first time *I* heard the phrase, of course, I do not remember. But for as long as I can remember this circle, this place where the sun does not set in spring, nor rise in winter, has been a call to my wandering hopes. Anything Arctic, from the Franklin expedition to the voyage of the *Nautilus*, from the Siberian land bridge to the work of Gontran de Poncins, from SRA cards to *National Geographic*, held a promise I made to myself to see something extraordinary, something beautiful as well as dangerous and hard.

This particular summer morning I step over the circle, then

back, then over it again. I walk to the edge of the gravel, look at the horizon, and spin a slow circle as I try to imagine the sun on the summer solstice. It would rise 47 degrees by midday, and at midnight it would kiss the horizon. It would not set. Instead, it would appear to tour the perimeter of the visible world. And I try to imagine a bit of space as well. I'm not sure why, perhaps because the Arctic Circle itself is a mathematical construct resulting from the calculation of the tilt of the planet (the earth tilts 23-1/2 degrees off the orbital plane; the Arctic and Antarctic Circles are 23-1/2 degrees away from the poles), but before I left home I wondered how far a second of longitude (measured east-west along a line of latitude), as in degrees and minutes and seconds on a map, might be. I knew it would be one thing at the equator, and then diminish as the globe moved toward the poles. Would it be possible, I wondered, to see a second? What I learned is that the math goes like this: One degree at the equator equals 69.172 statute miles, or 365,228.16 feet. One minute is 1/60 of a degree, or 6,087 feet (approximately one nautical mile). To figure the diminishing distance, use this formula: feet times cos(degrees). So, 6,087 times cos(66 degrees, 33 minutes) or 6,087 times 0.39795 = 2,422.32 feet. One second is 1/60 of a minute, and 1/60 of 2,422.32 is 40.37 feet. Forty and a little less than one-half feet. I've walked twice that distance away from the Jeep already.

Sitting on the grass a short way off the road, looking east, I try to imagine the seconds becoming minutes becoming degrees. I try to imagine the whole of the planet, crisscrossed with lines of latitude and longitude. And then I stop. The math explains the midnight sun in summer and the tremendous dark cold of winter. The math gives me a marker for my own desire. But I wonder, too, if there is anything in this math that tells me where I am.

If arrival can be said to be a physical feeling, that is, if a person can say, "I feel like I have arrived," then north of the circle, I am a very happy man. Anything, now, is possible.

Driving north from the circle, the roadway leaves the high

ground, crosses a valley, rises again into mountains and toward Wright Pass, the border between the Yukon and the Northwest Territories, and the third time I'll cross the continental divide on this road. But in the valley, two things happen.

First, it occurs to me that a compass, if I had one, would here be pointing more east than north. The north magnetic pole, which wanders a bit as the planet's magnetosphere shifts, was (last time I checked) at 79 deg 19 min north, 105 deg 26 min west, just off Ellef Ringnes Island, in Nunavut. Following the compass would put me on a line to Ellesmere Island, then Greenland, then through the North Sea and into Germany.

Second, a bear comes out of the brush and I do something stupid.

Lumbering, a fast walk or half trot, a red-brown bear—giant, I think; grizzly, I think—appears on the west shoulder of the road and begins to cross, heading away from me. Even though I'm on the black shale, I hit the brakes hard, and I can feel all four tires lock and skid. Backseat! I think. The camera bag—it's in the backseat! The car still sliding, I turn and start digging in the pile—the duffel bag, the jacket, the other pair of boots. The camera! I unzip the camera bag, rip the camera out, and turn to face front again. The bear is—where? Nothing. Not even a breeze moves the tops of the fireweed. Because the top is not on the Jeep today, I stand on the seat, camera ready, and scan the landscape east of the highway. Nothing. I wait. I sit back down, then put the camera on the passenger seat. The engine is still running. No air hisses from any tire. But I cannot leave. I look every direction. The bear, I am sure, is gone. My gut instinct, though—to turn away from the bear so I could get a damn picture of it; a trophy?—bothers me greatly. I don't care about the north magnetic pole anymore. All I want is the bear to come back. I'll leave the camera on the seat.

Soon enough, however, the sadness goes away. This valley, these mountains, this roadway, high tundra, muskeg valleys of jack pine and willow, it's all just so remarkably beautiful. The car goes in gear; I climb toward the pass.

At Wright Pass, the valleys both east and west are huge and alive with Arctic summer urgency. The wind is not gentle here, but I want to remain. This border, like all borders, seems to imply something I can never quite grasp. Something about physical space, or political history. I know what a divide is, but I want to feel it in the dirt. I know about provincial boundaries, but I do not know the people who made them.

The vista from the pass is stunning. But not untroubled. And it is the road itself that bothers me. There is a part of me that wants to kneel in thanks for the roadway, for the possibility that I might be here. And there is a part of me that cannot bear the sight of the seam. Conflicted, but happy, I drive downhill into the Northwest Territories.

James Creek passes through a culvert under the highway. A highway maintenance camp, chain-link fence, tin buildings, looking like every other highway shop in North America were it not for a mountain and clear stream as borders, sits back from the crossing on the west side. A small blue sign with a picture of a fish, however, points to a pullout on the east side—a gravel parking spot, then the rushing water. Not very deep. Not very far across. The rock streambed worn smooth here, then jagged a bit farther downstream. If they're going to put a sign up, I think, then I'm going to fish.

The thing about fly-fishing, of course, is to tie on a fly that matches the local bugs. Local bugs can change hourly, so it's always a challenge to find the right match. Here, in the Richardson Mountains, north of the Arctic Circle, I have no idea what might be in the stream, or how I might match it. So I tie on something called a Chernobyl ant, a huge foam and rubber imitation of a gargantuan black ant, cast it into the stream, and the grayling are hungry. I'm bringing the second one in when I realize there's a man standing behind me.

"Hello," I say.

He smiles and nods at me.

"Who are you?" I ask.

"Charlie," he says, walking closer.

I do not see any other car, but I ask him anyway. "Are you traveling the highway?"

"No," he says. "Survey crew." He points through some brush, and suddenly I see a trailer and a pickup truck forty, maybe fifty, yards away. "We're on break."

"Want to try?" I ask, holding the fly rod toward him.

"No," he says. But he does start talking. He asks about the hooks, and the line. He nods his head and smiles at every answer, and after a while he walks away. A few minutes later, another man, Charlie's partner, walks up. He's just as friendly, but does not talk as much. He simply wants to watch the fish. When he leaves, then Charlie comes back.

"Are you catching a lot?" he asks.

"Yes," I say. "Or the same one over and over."

"If you catch another one, can I have it?"

"Sure."

When I catch another one, I take it off the hook and hand it to him. He conks it over the head a couple of times with a stick and then carries it off to have lunch.

Before he leaves, though, I ask him how grayling taste, because I have read that they are a good eating fish. He says they taste wonderful. Just clean them, put them in a pan with some butter, and away you go. When I pass the both of them a short while later, Charlie standing twenty yards off the road's shoulder holding the surveying rod while his partner looks through the transit, we wave at each other like old friends.

North of James Creek the road leaves the mountains quickly and the land grows flat—bluffs and hills at the riverbanks, but otherwise a landscape of jack pine and muskeg. The water is tannic and slow. At the Peel River, the first of two ferry crossings, I wait as the white boat loads a car and a semi on the far side. The Peel River ferry is a cable ferry—a long steel cable strung between the two banks, a strong winch in the boat to pull it back and forth. Ramps at the bow and stern, though which is which changes with each trip. A white pilot's tower rises on the upriver side of the brown-and-red car deck.

When I get out of the Jeep, the man working as deckhand, directing the loading and unloading of traffic, walks up to me. He looks at my license plate and tries to rub off some of the dirt.

"Where're you from?" he asks.

"Minnesota," I say.

"Minnesota!" he calls up to the pilot, who takes a pencil and appears to write it down.

"Keeping a list?" I ask.

"Yeah."

"Anyone from Minnesota yet?"

"I just started a couple days ago. My list isn't very long."

As the boat begins to travel back across the river, the deckhand and I lean over the railing and watch the water swirl around the ferry's edges.

"Does this boat have propellers or just a winch?" I ask.

"Just the winch," he says.

"What happens if the cable breaks?"

"Well, it happened once," he says, turning to face me, and smiling a slow smile I know as well as my own—the smile that says it would really be something to see, eh? "The boat wound up a good bit downriver before it ran ashore."

The ferry across the Mackenzie River is a different story. Larger, propeller driven, the pilot's tower centered over the car-and-truck deck on a bridge of white steel, this ferry can hold a double-tandem semi and a good many cars. The Mackenzie River is the largest river in Canada. And where it meets the Arctic Red River, a much smaller stream coming in from the west, steep brown bluffs line both sides of the water. A town, which used to be called Arctic Red River, now called Tsiigehtchic, on the far side of its river namesake, appears almost quaint. The Catholic church, a red peaked roof with white walls and a bell spire, fronts the town on the river side. Homes, other buildings, fill the spaces away from the water.

As it turns out, I've shown up five minutes late. The ferry is midstream, chugging around the mouth of the Arctic Red toward the landing at Tsiigehtchic. From there it will motor across the Mackenzie, to the landing for the Dempster. Then it will return to the landing where I am now first in line. The ferry leaves only once an hour, so I have the time to rest, to walk around the riverbanks, then doze in the nighttime sunshine.

Hat down low over my eyes, I watch the ferry as it begins its trip from the far side of the Mackenzie. As it approaches, I hear the crunch of car tires on gravel, and then some more. People with better timing pull up behind me to get in line for the ride. The ferry off-loads the southbounders, then signals for us to drive on board. Pulling up to the far chain, I shut off the engine, get out of the Jeep, and join the other drivers at a railing. One of the deckhands, however, has discovered a problem.

A maroon Chevrolet Suburban, clearly very new, is leaking air from the right rear tire. The deckhand signals to the driver, and the man who gets out speaks very little English.

"They can fix this," the deckhand says, "on the other side of the river. But we should get a spare on here while we can."

The man looks at him. "Good," he says. The man reaches into the truck, pulls out the owner's manual, and hands it to the deckhand. The deckhand turns to the page where it shows the jack location, then looks in the back of the truck.

"Well, that figures," he says. "It's not where they say it will be."

Suddenly there are three or four of us inside and under the Suburban. We look under the rear floor mat. We look by the engine. We look behind the rear axle. Finally I find it, under a hatch over a wheel well. The deckhand takes the jack and begins to change the tire.

The driver looks on, helpless, but not unhappy.

"Hello," I say.

"Hello," he says. Another strong German accent.

"Are you enjoying your trip?"

"Aaah, yes!" he says, then puts his hand over his heart. "I am a young man. I come to this country. I am sixty-two now—too old, but I am a young man. I come to this country."

I smile at him, knowing exactly what he's getting at.

"I understand," I say. "Here every day is special."

Again, his hand goes over his heart. His eyes grow large, and he sighs. He says, "Yes, very special."

From the ferry landing to Inuvik, the highway is lit by midnight sun. The occasional loon floats in a melt pond; the plume of dry white dust still rises from behind my car.

Outside Inuvik, a town whose name means Place of Man, 127 kilometers beyond the ferry, the radio comes back on. Not long after that, the airport, and then pavement for the roads. Soon enough, a caribou burger and fries at a small restaurant and take-out place called To-Go's. Looking at the odometer in the Jeep, I see I'm only fifty miles short of three thousand miles from home.

Sitting outside on the deck in front of To-Go's, what I do not know is that tomorrow I will board a small plane that will carry me to Tuktoyaktuk. The pilot will buzz the sites of two crashes as well as the Distant Early Warning station, and we will see pingos as well as beluga whales from the air. In Tuktoyaktuk, an Inuit man will drive us around in a van, show us the Hotel Tuk Inn, let us get off at a gift shop, a mission church, and a type of earth-covered house from centuries before. Standing in front of this house, I will hear ZZ Top coming from a modern house a block away. And later, I will wade knee-deep in the Arctic Ocean's Beaufort Sea.

The day after tomorrow I will check out of Inuvik's Eskimo Inn and head south on the Dempster, racing away from pavement and radio and stoplights, racing away from the Place of Man. I will cross the ferries, visit the grayling in James Creek and the Ogilvie River. Coming around a corner, I will drive into a flock of ptarmigan that scatters, one not quickly enough, and in Eagle Plains a man will ask if I kept the bird and ate it. At the Arctic Circle, I will spend an hour alone, amazed at the size of the planet. In Eagle Plains I will eat a large meal, and smile because the hotel staff remembers me. But I will not spend the night. Instead, I will fill the gas tank and continue south, the light never fading. I will fish, and hike, and drive, and when I get to the Klondike Corner I will worry because it is closed, and I do not know if I have enough gas to get into Dawson. I'll make it, though, and I'll check into the Downtown Hotel, and the desk clerk will convince a cook to send me a supper and a bottle of Arctic Red beer.

What I do not know yet is that I will see a storm in the Tombstone Mountains, just a single rain cloud, moving east away from the road. And the rain that falls from it, lit by the low angle of the sun, will appear to be a rainbow. Not an arc, but a shimmering and cascading belt of color falling from cloud to sky. Red and blue and green and yellow and orange.

What I do know, however, is the length of one road. What I know is the connection between desire and joy. What I know is a few more stories. What I know, now, is that there are new spaces in my heart and mind, new ways of seeing sunlight and river water and bears that rise out of willows, new ways of seeing the mysterious made particular, hard, beautiful, and dangerous. And I know that the trip in front of me, the retracing of the exploration, will make each new story better, and allow me to bring them home.

ABOUT THE AUTHOR

W. Scott Olsen is professor of English at Concordia College in Moorhead, Minnesota, and editor of the literary journal *Ascent*. He is coauthor of *When We Say We're Home: A Quartet of Place and Memory* (The University of Utah Press, 1999), and coeditor of *The Sacred Place: Witnessing the Holy in the Physical World* (The University of Utah Press, 1996), and *A Year in Place* (The University of Utah Press, 2001).